Spread the Peanut Butter Thin!

by
Leah Bassinger Riley

PublishAmerica
Baltimore

© 2007 by Leah Bassinger Riley.
All rights reserved. No part of this book may be reproduced, stored in a retrieval system or transmitted in any form or by any means without the prior written permission of the publishers, except by a reviewer who may quote brief passages in a review to be printed in a newspaper, magazine or journal.

First printing

ISBN: 1-4241-8379-0
PUBLISHED BY PUBLISHAMERICA, LLLP
www.publishamerica.com
Baltimore

Printed in the United States of America

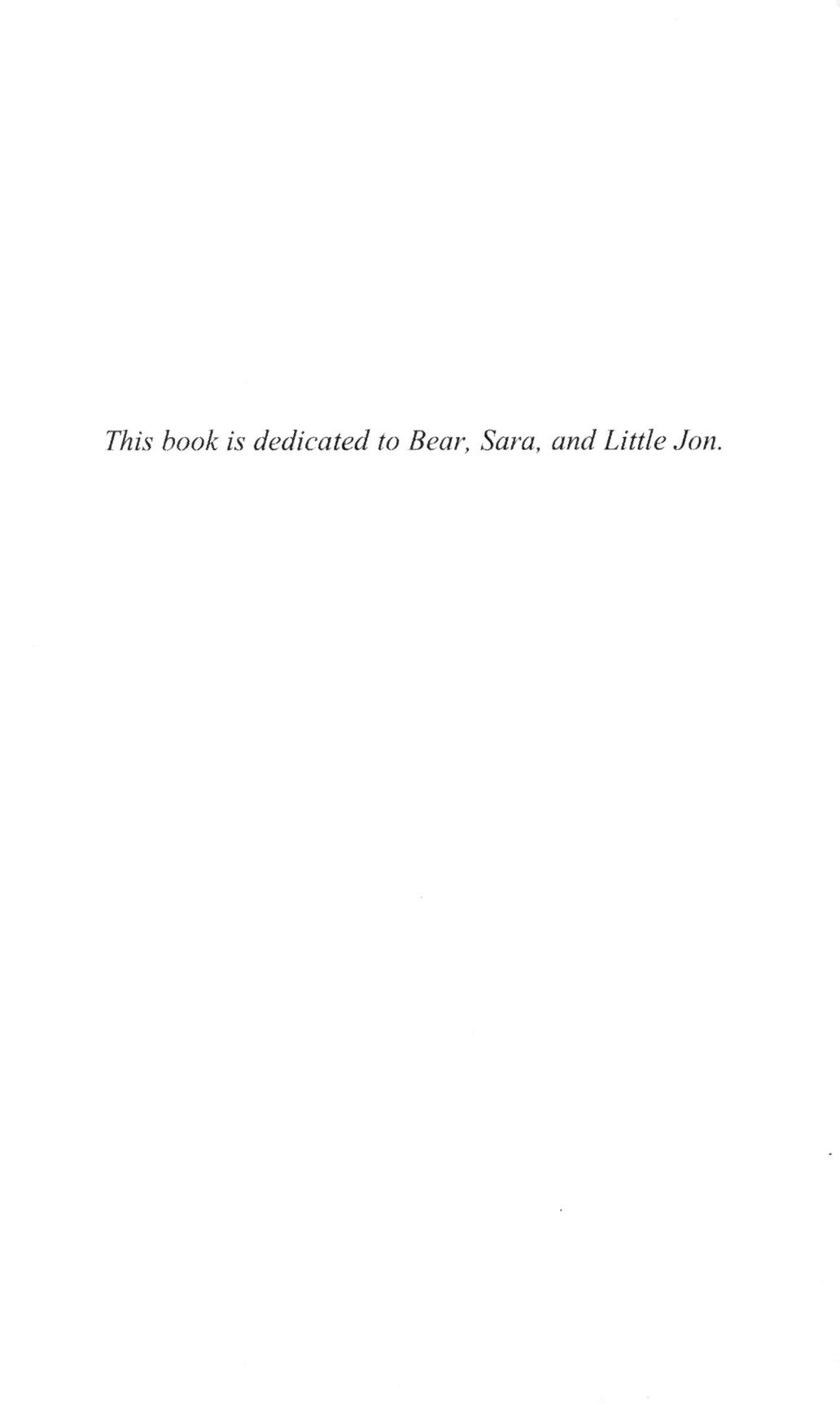

This book is dedicated to Bear, Sara, and Little Jon.

> To: Jim + Ida Strain
> Without you showing me Jesus I would not have been able to make it. Thank you!
> Leah

    I would like to acknowledge and thank the Lord Jesus Christ. Without His divine intervention and mercy on countless occasions, we would not have been able to endure. I would also like to thank the Strain family from Tulsa, Oklahoma. They invited me to Carbondale Baptist Church for vacation Bible school when I was a little girl. It was there that I got saved.

Preface

This is a book for everyone whose life is not always nice, happy, or comfortable. You know who you are. Maybe you are one of us, but are too afraid to admit it in your circle of overly-pleasant, syrupy-sweet, church friends. We are the Christians for whom life has grabbed by the throat, slammed into the wall, and punched between the eyes. We've been walked on, beaten when we're down, chewed up and spit out! We get irritated, angry and enraged. The *gnashing of teeth* isn't something that is only done in hell. We grind our teeth every night while we sleep! We have more important things to think about than what color the new carpet for the sanctuary will be, or what some blue-haired old lady said about the pastor last week. We are the ones that are tempted to steal money out of the collection plate! We live in the real world not some utopian mountain top. Yeah, we are the ones with *real* problems, lots of problems. What are *real* problems? Keep reading. You'll find out.

If you aren't a Christian, please feel welcome to continue reading. I am not perfect, far from it, don't pretend to be and I don't preach. I'm real. In fact, I am so far away from the stereotypical Christian that I'd bet some televangelist will have something bad to say about me if they read this. You know, I could probably say something about them too!

Seriously though, don't judge me until you've walked a mile in my hand-me-down shoes. Then again, I hope you never have to walk a whole mile in my shoes. Maybe if you just walked down the hallway in my shoes that would be enough. Even though I don't wish terrible things on anyone, if everyone could just walk a few steps in my shoes I believe there would be more understanding and empathy in the world. On the other hand, some of you might have walked much more than a mile in these crappy, worn out shoes. If that applies to you then I am truly sorry. My experiences will seem very trivial to you.

To those of you who are currently going through severe economic hardships, I hope this book helps you in some small way. Then again, the people that would get the most validation from our story will not be able to afford to buy the book. That said, no, this isn't a self-help book. This sure isn't a book on how to deal with your finances, be successful in life, raise your kids, or get rich. I loathe those books and the self-important people who write them!

Everything in this story is unfortunately true. I endeavored to record these events as completely as possible so that they may never be forgotten. I have my immediate family to back me up on that. Of course, they say that when a group of people witness an event they all remember things differently. I have tried to include as much input from my husband, daughter, and son as possible. This is their story as much as it is mine. We survived, just barely. This is a memoir of pain.

Some of the names in this book have been changed or intentionally omitted to protect identities.

Chapter One:
The Summer of 2004

When I was a little girl in Tulsa, Oklahoma, I dreamed of living in a warm, sunny location with palm trees, sand and the ocean. That green-eyed, freckled-face, redheaded, child, Lea Jane Bassinger, was all grown up now. The woman, Leah Riley, didn't live anywhere near that tropical paradise I had imagined as a child, not even close. Welcome to Illinois!

One of the things I like most about Illinois is that everything freezes over for a few months out of the year. The temperature can hit minus fifteen degrees and the wind chill is even lower! The ground becomes as hard as frozen slab of ribs. When it is that cold outside you wear your coat *inside* the house. I've even worn my coat to sleep in. My husband, Jon, also known as Big Jon or Bear, has worn up to seven shirts at the same time trying to keep warm. Exposed skin can freeze in a matter of minutes. The sensation you feel is like bazillions of tiny, razor-sharp knives cutting and burning you with a cold burn. Winter can dry your skin out so bad that it flakes, cracks and bleeds. Sometimes your lips get so chapped that you can't even open your mouth, let alone smile or talk, unless you grease your lips first with some kind of lip balm.

How do I find anything desirable about this godforsaken frozen wasteland? During winter, mold, mildew and other forms of funk don't grow as fast. Our basement is wet, damp, moldy and gross! Basement slime smells awful!

At one point, the overpowering odor seeping up from my basement had the distinctive sickly sweet smell of road kill. The basement smelled like a dead body! No, it was more like a thousand road kills had been placed in my basement. I could imagine the rotting, bloated bodies of opossums, raccoons, dead cats and someone's lost dog all hidden away in the corner of my basement by some sicko freak that had just escaped from the correctional center. The flies had surely found the yet unseen dead bodies in my basement by now. The maggots would be squirming around in masses just under the skin of the deceased trying to find a way out. Any tear in the skin would be followed by the trickle of foul smelling juices dripping from the remains. The larvae would emerge from the ripe carcasses sooner or later and wriggle away on the hard, cold, basement floor in search of the next host. Then there would be nothing left, but a pile of fur and sticky ooze. The thought was appalling. If I didn't go down there, eventually the carcasses would dry up. Ultimately, the only trace evidence remaining would be a little hair stuck to the bones and a pile of dehydrated worms. Come to think of it, Michael Angelo, our gray and white male cat, hadn't been home in about two weeks. Hmm…

I quickly summoned my cats for a head count by rattling their bag of dry food. Cats came running up to me from all directions with anticipation. Their meowing grew louder as they tumbled over themselves trying to vie for position. I tried to take a step forward, but tripped on a cat. My attempts to limit the cat population around our house had obviously failed long ago. In the country there are many people who have five, six, or even a dozen or more cats. They are known as farm cats or barn cats. Most of these types of cats are feral. Now let's see, how many cats do we have currently? Was it 12, 13, 14?

Some cats were still missing. I slowly shuffled my feet around the assembled cats as I made my way to the end of the carport. I "meowed" in my best cat voice. One more came running in from the yard. "Where are you cats? Meow?" After several minutes of calling cats I spied the last cat. It was lying down on top of the carport watching me meowing and making a fool out of myself. Ok, well at least it wasn't one of them that I smelled in my basement.

The time had come to act. It had been a long time since I had been down in the basement. Perhaps some homeless person had snuck in while we were gone one evening and had died there. Eew! What a horrible way to die! They must have succumbed to the choking mold and mildew. Perhaps they were attacked by one of the giant wolf spiders that inhabit the dark recesses of our underground abyss. This is crazy! We live out in the middle of nowhere Illinois, commonly referred to as B.F.E. by one of my daughter's friends who lived in Bolivia. We have three neighbors. It was miles to the nearest town of any size. No, it couldn't be a homeless person.

What is that putrid smell then? The tangy sweet smell of death was overwhelming. I did the only thing I could do. I sent Big Jon and Little Jon, now a tall, broad-shouldered fourteen year old boy, down to investigate with a mandate that they start dragging everything outside and burning it. Cleaning out the basement was long over due. First, the males would need some sort of protective mask. We never clean anything without first donning a dust mask. Not wearing a mask was suicidal.

Our house used to be clean once. This was long ago when we first moved here. I was a stay-at-home mom then. I home-schooled my kids and even had a little music studio in my living room where I taught private lessons. We cleaned every day, for three or four hours a day, back then. Our house was magazine perfect in those days. That has been so long ago now that my kids don't remember those times. Now all my kids remember is dust, mold, clutter, and stench. They are also keenly aware of the severe allergies and asphyxiating asthma that accompany these unsanitary conditions. Yes, we had become slobs.

We had a huge task at hand. The excavation of the basement was about to commence. This isn't routine cleaning. It is *excavation*. This is not a job for the females in the house. Sara, a petite seventeen-year-old, and I exempted ourselves from the matter. In fact, we excluded ourselves from any job that is too disgusting or revolting. I assigned Sara to painting the back porch. I, on the other hand, did not have the time to engage in many of the house excavating chores because I was always at work. Every day before I left for work I would leave a list of things that needed to be done and assign each item to either Sara, My Bear, or Little Jon. Some things would never get done.

Painting the back porch seemed simple enough. Nothing is ever simple around our house. Even buying the paint wasn't simple. I was bringing home $1,200.00 a month as a debt collector and had an $800.00 mortgage payment. Jon was bringing home about $75.00 every other week from his job at Hardees during this particular time. If you factor in gasoline, food, electric, and phone, there isn't much left over for frivolities like paint. Nevertheless, we had a goal. We were going to clean up this pit and make it look as nice as possible. I had always wanted to use our enclosed back porch as a little breakfast room. I envisioned it with pretty patio furniture and potted houseplants. It was an incredibly messy storage area and home to many spiders. This was a far cry from when I was a stay-at-home mom and used to mop the back porch several times a day. I mopped it every time a child came or left for a music lesson. Now, the back porch hadn't been swept or mopped regularly in years.

I selected a bright yellow paint for the walls and dark green trim for the windows and doors. Bright yellow and green just happen to be the color of John Deere tractors. We were toying with the idea of hanging up pictures of tractors and calling it the tractor room. Sara detested anything country, while I loved country living. We dismissed the tractor décor idea and went for sunflowers. Sara hand painted some sunflowers on the sides and above the door leading to the kitchen. The back porch was not enclosed originally. At one point in time, someone enclosed it, but left the blue, outdoor siding on the interior walls. The rest of the house had tan-colored siding. It was obvious that our house was pieced together, one room at a time, by the former owners that lived there.

The paint was supposed to cover the area with one coat. We were painting over outdoor siding that just happened to be indoors, so it took two coats to cover it completely. Two coats meant twice the price. Sara suggested we complain about the paint and get our money back. Later on, she discovered a warning on the paint that stated it was to be used in a well-ventilated area with a mask. The store employee who had mixed the paint had painted over this warning! Sara and Little Jon thought we should sue. Ever since Little Jon had heard about ridicules lawsuits that had made people rich he was always on the lookout for a good claim. It isn't that we wanted to ruin other people's lives with a stupid lawsuit. We just wanted to improve ours. I was the reigning poster child for college doesn't pay and work pays even less. Somehow in this nation's current economic decline, the rules had changed. Education and hard work didn't mean what they used to. In fact, they didn't mean much at all. My kids were creatively trying to come up with ways to survive in an economy of boarded up businesses and jobs that don't pay enough to provide even the most basic human needs.

We also decided to paint the steps going down to the basement yellow and purple in keeping with the local high school's colors. In a hard to reach location, above the door leading to the basement, Sara had painstakingly stenciled, "Tornado Ally", since this is where we go when tornados strike. She did a beautiful job and it was almost a shame to mention it, but I couldn't let Sara's dyslexia have a permanent monument in my home. Much to her disappointment, I informed Sara that she needed to change "ally" to "alley." The Taylorville High School mascot is a tornado so, Sara carefully painted the likeness of "Tommy the Tornado" on the wall of the stairway. The back porch and the stairs turned out very nicely. The paint fumes were very strong and masked most of the rotting odor coming up from the basement.

The basement stench had seemed to mysteriously lessen and then disappear altogether. I attributed this to the fact that the males had been burning large piles of soggy debris from the basement for several days now. There was a mildewed tent, a box of molded children's books, and heaps of every manner of rotten garbage, which at one time were cherished or useful items. When we had moved into the house several years ago, we discovered that the basement leaked. Then, we discovered that we had active termites! The inspection had said we didn't have termites. When we had the house treated for termites, the holes they drilled in the basement turned the tiny leaks into large, cascading waterfalls that streamed down the walls every time it rained. This almost constant moisture and lack of air conditioning in the warmer months caused anything that was in the basement to disintegrate into a damp, greenish, furry, mold.

Just as mysteriously as the disgusting smell had disappeared, it was back in full force. It had to be the septic! The septic water must be draining into the basement! The basement didn't smell like raw sewage though. This is what had thrown us off track. It seriously smelled like a dead body! Nevertheless, that was the only thing it could be. Earlier this summer, we had finally opened the windows because it had been too hot inside the house. We had noticed then that septic was running out on top of the ground. Terrific! Here was another thing we couldn't afford to fix. Just to get the septic pumped, so we could figure out what was wrong with it, would cost about $120.00 dollars. Jon had no knowledge of septic repair. It didn't matter even if he knew how to fix it. I couldn't afford the materials to do-it-yourself. Repairing the septic just wasn't going to happen unless I won the lottery or some magical money fairy visited us. I never played the state lotto. I couldn't afford that either. However, the Publisher's Clearing House online lotto was free and I played it religiously. I never won.

The septic was directly outside my bedroom window. Jon and I could either close the window and die of heat stroke or we could deal with smelling our own urine and feces every night. Neither choice was acceptable. We opted for opening the window and enjoying the *sweet country air*. Actually, the raw sewage wasn't too bad when the wind wasn't blowing. Other times, it was so powerful that it would sting the insides of my nostrils. I was only in my bedroom to sleep. After I fell asleep I would smell nothing. This was my theory anyway. My theory was incorrect. I would be fully asleep and yet very aware of the foul fumes. Jon was lucky. He had a CPAP machine he used for his sleep apnea at night. It is basically a little mask that fits over his nose and forces air constantly into his airway so he doesn't snore or intermittently quit breathing. The CPAP filtered out the smell for him.

As the summer progressed, more and more sewage collected on top of the ground. Now, the smell was constant whether the wind blew or not. Jon dug a small canal to drain the stagnant sewage away from the house and further out into the yard. We'd have to make do.

Not only did everything in the basement mold over, but a lot of things in the house molded over too, especially in the closets. There's nothing like having to throw away a perfectly good purse or a pair of shoes because they are covered in mold spots that refuse to be cleaned. The mold also grew on the outside of the many musical instrument cases I had. Sometimes the mold actually grew inside the cases and on the instruments themselves! The mold inside the house came from the windows being left open constantly during the summer months because we had no air conditioning. The air conditioning died about two years after we moved in and we didn't have money to get it fixed or replaced. Having large holes in our roof, battle scars from a small tornado that never really touched the ground, didn't help either. Apparently, this little whirlwind must have decided to stay several feet off the ground. Even so, it was still able to rip several large branches off some of the many trees that surround our house. We were so poor at the time, we took the insurance money that was meant to fix our roof and spent it on other, more pressing concerns such as groceries, car insurance and the like.

Jon fixed the roof himself. I use the word "fix" very loosely. My Bear was not trained as a carpenter, electrician, plumber, or in any other manual labor field. He had to learn about these things only because we could no longer afford to pay a professional to do them for us. Bear really didn't have anyone he could ask for help so he learned what he could from the people at the hardware store and from books. Reading books and talking to people is *not* the best way to learn a hands on activity. However, this is what Jon had to do. Our other option was to simply leave the branches sticking in our roof. They were in there tight. I doubt the rain could have leaked in if we just left them as they were. Nah, It would have looked too stupid.

There were several branches of various sizes, from three inches to ten inches in diameter. I went up into the attic to take a look. Have you ever seen those horror movies where the killer is trying to stab someone on the other side of a door? Usually, there is some bimbo on one side of the door unable, or too stupid, to move. All the while, the evil psycho freak in the black hood is stabbing long, bloody knives through the door, just barely missing the intended victim. Our roof, from inside our attic roof, looked like Mr. Killer had been there and had tried repeatedly to stab us with tree branches.

First, Bear pulled out the tree limbs that were piercing our roof. We now had several mini, jagged, *skylights*. Then, Bear crawled up in the attic and nailed pieces of plywood to the inside of our attic roof. Great! At this point, we had nails sticking pointed side up on the outside of our roof. Next, my bear climbed on top of the roof and covered the plywood patches with white caulk. Our brown roof now had white blotches all over it. There was one consolation. This was the back side of the house that no one saw. I was watching my beloved home fall into disrepair before my eyes.

Some time later, we discovered that Jon's marvelous patchwork hadn't held and we had water coming in through the roof. Bear patched it again with globs of sticky, black, tarry stuff. This time it held. The roof looked pretty *ghetto,* but we were the only ones that were going to see it so it didn't matter. We had quit entertaining guests long ago. Time and money didn't permit inviting visitors over any more. I couldn't afford to feed my own family much less offer a meal to a friend. When was I supposed to do all this entertaining anyway? Working two and three jobs simultaneously hardly left time for basic cleaning let alone the deep cleaning that was needed for company. Believe me, this house needed much more than a light touch up or surface cleaning!

It's interesting how when I was in college and then started working full time, plus jobs on the side, that nothing ever got cleaned any more around here. Imagine that. I learned that you have to actually be at home sometime in order to clean your house. Jon was an incompetent when it came to cleaning. He once tried to clean the toilet with a bar of dial soap! He proceeded to clean the bathroom sink with the toilet brush! What can I say? He always had maids when he was growing up! Welcome to the real world! We had many heated *discussions* regarding the need to clean.

"If the department of child and family services came out here they would put our kids in foster care because this house is so filthy!" I screamed.

"You are exaggerating. There are other people that have worse houses than this," Jon stated, unmoved.

"I don't care about other people. I can't even come home and cook anything because there isn't a clean pot to cook in. If I *was* able to find a clean pot there are no clean dishes to eat off of and it would take an hour to unearth the kitchen table because there is so much crap on top of it," I yelled.

Jon challenged, "Then why don't you do something about it?"

"Why don't YOU do something? I work twice as many hours as you do. I always have!"

"That's not true!" Jon said defensively.

"It has been for the last several years!" I seethed, feeling my blood boil.

"Then get the kids to do something," Jon suggested, unwilling to take responsibility.

"The kids *do* help me on weekends when they don't have school work. They both have learning disabilities and you know it takes Sara three times longer than the average student to do her homework. You should have been helping Little Jon the whole time I was in college with his schoolwork. You wouldn't even do that! That's why he got left back in third grade! I couldn't be here to help him with his schoolwork because I had schoolwork of my own! Start picking up the crap off the floor! Sara, grab a broom! Little Jon, take out this trash!"

The proverbial *shit* had hit the fan. Mom had exploded! The kids were running quickly to find long unused brooms and trash bags, of which the whereabouts were unknown. Big Jon was hurriedly picking up trash off the floor. Yes, there was trash strewn all over the floor! It was that bad!

"Why do I have to start yelling like this to get you people to do anything around here?!" I questioned angrily. I wasn't quite finished lecturing, but the harshness of my tone had lessened now that everyone had started cleaning.

"Well..." Big Jon started.

"I don't want a response. Keep working!" I snapped.

"Why can't you just take the initiative and do things without me having to ask you to do them?" I continued, not wanting to leave anything unsaid.

There was no response this time, only a fuming look from Jon.

"Because..." Little Jon began.

"You stay out of it!" I warned.

"I have to do all the work around here because these lazy males never do anything!" Sara piped up.

"You better shut up if you know what's good for you," Big Jon growled.

"I will not shut up. It's the truth! They never do anything!" Sara said defiantly.

"Stop it! Walk away. Don't escalate it!" I ordered Big Jon.

"She's the one that started it!" he said childishly.

"You are *supposed* to be an adult! I feel like I'm a single mom with three kids and you are my teenage son!" I said in frustration.

Thank God we live in the country and not in one of those stuck-up cookie cutter neighborhoods in the city. If this house was in the city where there are neighborhood associations we would have been fined a million times over for the condition of our house, both inside and out. We were living worse than animals!

Chapter Two:
The Beginning of Tragedy

How did a regularly tithing, church-going, former home-schooling family sink to this level? What went wrong? All our problems started in 1996 when we first moved in to our wonderful countryside home. I had wanted a house in the country all my life! Well, when I wasn't dreaming of my *Gilligan's Island* fantasy home with the beach, anyway. I had been addicted to the books by Laura Wilder, and later on, the television show, *Little House on the Prairie,* as a child. What can I say? I loved the idea of having lots of land, animals, a huge garden, nature all around, and few to no neighbors.

Jon would say our problems started long before we moved here. I suppose if you take into account that Jon was constantly being laid off from one job to the next, and that he had to take contract computer programming jobs, which only lasted a few months at a stretch, maybe we had it bad all along.

Every time one of his contract jobs ended, we would pack up the U-

Haul truck and move our household across the country, following the next job. I didn't see this as a problem, just the opposite. I was very eager and excited to move, see new places, and find out how other people lived. Ever since I was eight years old I yearned to go on vacations and see something I hadn't seen before. I would have done anything to be able to see a real live palm tree and go swimming in the ocean, or go swimming anywhere at all. My childhood family, due to poverty, hadn't been able to satisfy my youthful desire to travel. Now, moving all the time was like vacationing in a way, only we got to stay longer. I was making up for lost time and finally getting to see a little bit of the country. I home-schooled my kids so it wasn't like they were being uprooted from their schools and teachers. After all, I was showing my kids places I had never dreamed of going. We did leave behind friends, but I was young and had a lust for travel.

In between jobs, Jon didn't draw an income so we had to use credit cards to pay for necessities like food, car repairs, etcetera. We always caught up on the credit cards when he got his next assignment. Paying for all the moving expenses did add up though.

As I said, our real problems didn't start until 1996. We had finally found the home of our dreams. We moved in and about a week later Jon got fired because he fell asleep at work. He didn't only fall asleep, but they heard him snoring in a conference room down the hall. He would never work as a computer programmer again. Jon blamed the loss of his career as a programmer on sleep apnea and an undiagnosed narcoleptic sleep disorder. He had fallen asleep while driving numerous times so this wasn't an entirely invalid claim. I blamed it on the fact that he didn't discipline himself to go to bed at a decent hour. It was probably a combination of both.

Now, with the family breadwinner wallowing in depression, self-pity and joblessness, it was up to me to do something. What could I do? I didn't have any marketable skills that would earn enough to support a family of four. I couldn't make the payments on this house we had just moved into by myself.

I didn't have a college education. This was the key. I had always been told to get an education and then I would have a better life. It isn't that I didn't try to get an education when I graduated from high school. The cards were stacked against me when I was eighteen. In December of 1981, my father started limping and walking with a cane. He was seventy-six years old and my mother thought that he simply was getting old. My father was never one to go to a doctor and this time was no different. He merely grabbed his cane and went to work every day in the men's department at the Froug's department store, in West Tulsa, where he was an assistant manager. As the months wore on he cut back to part time hours. Barbara, my sister, came home to visit from Oklahoma City where she had been living. Barbara was a nurse and apparently she could tell that he needed to be in the hospital. He was in the hospital for a few days while they did tests. I don't think he ever knew what was wrong with him. We went up to visit him once. The nurse was changing the sheets or something and moving him around. He was in a lot of pain and probably on some major painkillers. He yelled out my name, "Lea! Lea!" Then, I think he mumbled, "Take it easy" or "Stop it." He evidently thought that I was the one who was touching him and causing the pain. I didn't want him to think I was the one manhandling him. I didn't want that to be his last memory of me. We decided to leave the room until the nurse got finished. I don't remember going back.

Apparently, his body was eaten up with cancer. They had no idea of telling exactly where the cancer had started. I assumed it had started as lung cancer. He had smoked from the time he was sixteen years old. On April 15, 1982, we received a call from the hospital. I was getting ready to go to school. I answered the phone. Earl Elbert Bassinger was dead. Not too long after that call, my friend Mary Alley called. I'm not sure what she had wanted. I told her that my father had "croaked." Maybe that was my way of trying to be strong, like this sort of thing happens and it's not that big of a deal. I can handle it. It's alright. Mary thought I was just playing around. She didn't think that he was really dead. Perhaps, my choice of words wasn't the best. Several days later, I found the time, when no one would see or hear me, to lock myself in the bathroom and cry. Highly charged emotions were uncomfortable and awkward for my family.

My father had died about four weeks before my graduation from Webster High School. Consequently, I don't remember much about the actual graduation ceremony. They must have called my name, Lea Jane Bassinger, when it was time to receive my diploma. I probably walked across a stage, smiled and shook someone's hand. Was the high school band there to play "Pomp and Circumstance" or was it even played at all? Did I have a cake afterwards? Surely, I had been given some kind of graduation present from someone. I do know the graduation was held at Oral Roberts University and that my oldest sister Catherine, my Mother and Barbara were there. I remember they made me stand against a wall with my diploma while they took a picture. I don't remember anything else.

It was during my senior year in high school, right around the time that my father died, that I developed anxiety or panic attacks. The first attack I had was while I was taking a shower. I thought the water in the shower was too hot. Maybe I was just overheated. My heart started pounding. I got out of the shower and sat on the end of my bed in a towel trying to catch my breath, cool down and calm myself. While I was sitting there naked, my friend Mary, from across the street, came over. I was immediately distracted from my symptoms. I hurriedly threw on some clothes and tried not to look feeble. My heart was still racing a little, but I kept telling myself, silently, to get over it. Fifteen minutes later, my heart rate was back to normal.

Neither of my parents had money. They were quite poor. Nevertheless, I had been working at a T.G.&Y., five and dime store, since I was sixteen and had saved up a little money to go to college. I had enough saved to pay for about one year of college. I tried to go to the University of Oklahoma, but I was anything but focused on my studies.

The only thing I could really concentrate on at OU was my job in the cafeteria. The work was methodical, repetitive and brainless. My job was to scrape the leftover food off plates, pour out the discarded beverages from the student's glasses and dump everything into a huge trash can. The inside of the trash can was a mix of liquified food particles. It looked like a big bucket of puke. Then, I'd stack the dirty plates, cups and silverware so they could be taken to the dishwasher. It was a nasty job and occasionally I'd get a little of the slop splashed on me, but I didn't mind.

    My grades, however, reflected my emotional status. I continued to have panic attacks while at OU. One attack occurred during an orchestra rehearsal. I had to tap the first chair violist on the shoulder and tell her I thought there was something wrong with my heart. She packed up her instrument and drove me over to the university clinic. I thought I was definitely going to die this time. I felt as if I would pass out. I blamed myself. I had had too much caffeine recently. That must have been it. The doctor agreed that caffeine was the culprit. After about thirty minutes at the clinic I was shaky, but otherwise fine. My fellow violist escorted me back to my dorm room. I tried to relax from my seemingly near death experience and managed to sleep through the night. I was now extremely afraid to ingest anything containing caffeine and I'd keep this unfounded fear of caffeine for the next several years.

    Another panic attack happened when I had gone home from college to visit my mother. This time I hadn't had a drop of caffeine in weeks. I suddenly started having rapid heart palpitations for no obvious reason. It hadn't been the caffeine. Or was I suffering withdrawals? No, I must have a heart problem. The lights in the room started to dim. Objects looked far away. I felt exhausted. I had to lie down on the sofa in the living room. My mother was blind by this time, but I needed her to be able to call an ambulance. We had an old rotary phone. She could feel the bar where the zero was and count her way around the dial to find the other numbers. I told my mother that I thought I was dying. I wanted her to wait and check on me to see if I got any worse before she called for help. She seemed concerned, but not overly alarmed. I don't know what I expected. I suppose I was thinking that the ambulance would get there in time to resuscitate me should my heart stop completely. I was lying on the couch taking my pulse rate constantly. It was beating faster than if I had been running several laps around a track. I recovered, inexplicably, in about an hour.

    I rarely went home to visit except on holidays when the dorms were closed. I liked my freedom as any young adult would, probably more than most. My mother had been overprotective while I was growing up. In high school I had not been allowed to date at all. Going to a school dance was out of the question. I supposed she was trying to keep me from getting pregnant. She rejected the thought of teenage girls wearing make-up or shaving their legs. I never cared much for make-up, but hairy legs?! I had not been at liberty to even go to the mall or to a movie with female friends. I guess she thought we'd try to pick up boys. Riding in a car with another teenager was banned at all times. Driving the family car was prohibited. She was, no doubt, trying to keep me from being in a car wreck. My parents never carried medical insurance on me while I was growing up. One medical mishap might have meant bankruptcy for them. My father drove me everywhere I needed to go and picked me up when I was done. Staying at home alone, even at the age of seventeen or eighteen was outlawed. Was she afraid that the big bad wolf might come to the door? I was also not permitted to go to a single slumber party as a child. Did she think that my best friend's dad would try to rape me or something? No. More likely, it was that little girls tend to talk about make-up and boys at slumber parties. My mother didn't even want me to ride my bicycle around the block, at the age of thirteen, because she couldn't "see" me. She must have been afraid of child abductors.

My mother gave me the impression that she didn't want me to grow up and that this was in some way a bad thing. I was the baby of the family. I'm sure that had something to do with it. She had grown up in Brooklyn from the age of ten to around age twenty. Had some of these terrible things happened to her? I don't know. Maybe she had seen these things happen to other people while living in New York. We weren't in the crime-ridden city streets of New York. We were in laid back Tulsa, Oklahoma of the 1970's!

Most of the other kids, including my roommate, at OU would go home every weekend. On Thanksgiving and Christmas there would be turkeys and hams awaiting them. If I went home there would be no home-cooked meal waiting for me. My mother was too sick for that.

Meals on Wheels brought food to her every day at noon. She'd let me eat some of it. Frequently, I'd take her over to McDonald's and we'd get one of their twenty-five cent hamburger specials.

The other kid's moms would do their laundry for them, buy them special things and send them back with huge care packages full of all kinds of treats. I had to do my mother's laundry. No one would be doing *my* laundry. It was certain that I wouldn't be toting a basket of toiletries and home-baked cookies with me when I returned to OU. I wasn't jealous as much as I was sad.

The other young adult's dads would give them spending money, pay their car insurance, and take care of any bills they had from school. I didn't have a father anymore. I took care of my own car insurance. I paid for my tuition and any other bills with my part time job at the cafeteria on campus.

The Christmas of 1982 was depressing. I had set up our Christmas tree and decorated it on my own. I tried to act happy, as if nothing was wrong. I figured there wouldn't be any presents this year. My father had died last April and without his small paycheck my mom only had her social security to live on. Even if she would have had any money, she was blind and couldn't see to go shopping. Besides, she didn't leave the house much anymore since my father wasn't around to drive her anywhere. Mainly, she only went to doctor appointments now. I knew I was an adult and shouldn't want gifts, especially with money the way it was. Christmas is for little kids. I hated myself for being so babyish. The Christmas spirit wasn't about getting; it was about Jesus being born. Christmas was about giving and joy. I kept thinking about the Dr. Seuss book, *How the Grinch Stole Christmas*. The Grinch hadn't been able to stop Christmas from coming, even though he took all the gifts, decorations and even the food. I admired the Whos down in Whoville when they got up Christmas morning and began to sing Christmas carols despite the fact that they had nothing tangible to celebrate with. Why couldn't I be the better person, the adult, the mature individual and just recognize the holiday for its religious significance. Other people had gone through rough times before. I wasn't the only one. I bet they didn't agonize over not getting presents on Christmas. My best friend, Christy, and her husband didn't have the money to give each other presents this year either. She had tried to reason with her husband that they should at least have one small present a piece. He hadn't even wanted to do that. She was disappointed, but *she* took it like a grown-up. I was going to have to snap out of it. Who did I think I was anyway? There are people in Africa that are literally dying from starvation and I want a Christmas present!? My mother always told me, "You are growing up, not down", whenever I acted childish. I wasn't going to let her see me being dejected about something so trivial.

I loaded up the dirty clothes into my father's baby blue Mercury Monarch and drove to the laundromat by myself. I was miserable. I filled the machines with dirty clothes, added soap, and started putting in the quarters. There was no one else in the laundromat except for an old, gray-haired lady. We didn't speak to each other. She finished her laundry and was on her way out. She stopped by the washing machine that I was bent over unloading. "You're too young to know that everything eventually turns out all right," she said to me.

Had she seen my sadness? How had she known? The dejection must have been oozing out of my pores!

After my first semester I couldn't handle living in the freshmen dorms any more. My roommate, Kelly, had never done laundry in her life. I had to teach her how to put the quarters in the machine one weekend when she couldn't go home and had to stay at the university to study. When she moved in, her mother, father and brother had all been there to help her. I had no one with me. She carried in load after load of clothes and other items. Her closet was crammed full. Those were just her summer clothes! All the clothes I owned, winter and summer, fit nicely into half of my closet. Kelly even brought her own chair. The university supplied a chair and a desk for each student. Apparently the chair that was supplied wasn't good enough for her. She had to have a huge wicker chair. Okay, maybe I was a little jealous, not of her abundance of material things, but of her parents and seemingly untroubled life. However, I *wasn't* envious of her portly physique. Then again, I wasn't her first choice for a roommate either. She had wanted to room with one of her friends from high school. I was more than happy to let her friend have my spot.

Second semester, I marched myself down to the housing office and demanded a room with the upperclassmen on the other side of campus. I was sick of carefree, immature children. I moved into an international student's dorm. The students here were a lot older than I. They came from every place on the globe. My new roommate, Mai, was 29 years old and from Viet Nam. There were many Vietnamese students there. Another friend I made there was from Nigeria. His name was Peter. Diane was part French and part Korean. She came from Hawaii. I learned a lot living in that environment. Most of the *men* and *women*, not children, in this building had parents overseas. They were on their own like I was. This was a much improved location for me.

I had my first taste of tofu and loved it. Much to Mai's alarm, the tofu I was eating happened to be rotten. I didn't know what it was supposed to taste like. I thought it was good, kind of tangy. I learned that agar makes a really firm Jell-O. I had never heard of agar before. Barbara told me that it was something they used in biology labs to grow bacteria in. I learned that eggs wouldn't necessarily spoil if you don't refrigerate them. Mai never refrigerated hers. I also realized that Asians ate unhatched eggs with baby chickens in them! I was disgusted! Mai had one of these eggs. I told her in no uncertain terms of my repulsion. She said, "Only men eat these kind of eggs and only when they are drunk." She had probably intended to eat it herself until my display of negative peer pressure won out.

I shopped at my first Asian grocery store. It smelled very different in there; a mixture of spoiled food with a twist of a farmer's feed store scent. The aroma was not appetizing in particular. Everything was new to me. There were so many interesting food items. I often didn't know if the things for sale were plants or animal products. Gluten was one of those things that I couldn't tell if it was plant or animal. It had the texture and taste of meat, but it sure didn't look like any meat I knew about. I fell in love with the canned, vegetarian chop suey with its tiny quail eggs, gluten, straw mushrooms, bamboo shoots and completely unfamiliar taste. I also enjoyed the sweet Chinese sausage and chicken cooked with sugar. Asians put sugar on their meat. Americans put salt on their meat. Culinarily speaking, it was like I had landed on a different planet. I had no prior knowledge of what anything might taste like, how to prepare it, or even if it was edible. I had even more weird and wonderful food at my first Chinese New Year's party.

I quit college after my freshman year at OU and moved back home to take care of my mother. In my mind I was an academic failure. I felt stupid. I thought there was something wrong with me and that I couldn't cut it on a college level. My high school transcript had A's, B's and National Honor Society written all over it; yet, somehow, I surely must be intellectually inferior. I said goodbye to my college career, my future, and my young adulthood with deep despair.

At age nineteen I became my mother's caregiver. I cleaned the house, did the laundry, went to the grocery store, paid the bills, gave my mother her many medicines, took her to doctor visits, cleaned up her tarry poop and pee from her bedside potty and fixed meals. I was probably the least equipped for the job. I had no experience or training as a caregiver. I hadn't even been allowed to babysit when I was growing up. I couldn't cook and had no idea that she was supposed to have been on a diabetic diet all these years. I didn't know what a diabetic diet was! To me, the definition of *diet* was something that fat people did. I had no medical experience. Catherine came by after work and checked on things a couple of times a week. Sometimes, Catherine took Mama to the doctor. Usually, Catherine yelled at me for being so stupid.

"Leah, she can't have barbeque sauce, it's loaded with sugar!" Catherine screeched.

"I didn't know," I answered stupidly. I had just *discovered* barbeque sauce. I thought it was great! Barbara had loved the taste of barbeque so much that she would eat the sauce plain, with no meat, on a piece of white bread. I really *didn't* know there was a lot of sugar in barbeque.

"You gave her the wrong dosage of potassium, are you trying to kill her, Leah?" Catherine was completely unsympathetic of my ignorance. How was I supposed to know the dosage had changed? I hadn't been the one that took her to the doctor last. I gave her the dosage that was written on the bottle. Besides, I was still getting used to the idea that Mama had to have someone take care of her now. I was used to Mama always taking care of me. It hadn't really donned on me that I had to be constantly aware of her every need.

Whenever Catherine asked me a question my answer would always be, "I don't know." Even if I had an opinion, or thought I knew the answer, I'd still answer her, "I don't know." I was thoroughly depressed and scared from seeing my mother's declining condition. I guess I thought if I *didn't know*, then I wouldn't be in trouble and she wouldn't chew me out. I'm sure Catherine got sick of my feigned, although sometimes genuine, lack of knowledge.

"Don't you know anything?" Catherine demanded.

She was right. Maybe I didn't know anything. That proved it. I had *gone stupid* after high school. I had noticed, on several occasions, where I had lacked the common sense to solve simple problems lately. I obviously had made a mistake in thinking that I would make it through college. After all, Barbara had even told me, way before I enrolled at OU, that a lot of the people who did well in high school had flunked out when they went to college. I didn't answer Catherine. I just shrugged my shoulders, not wanting to be verbally assaulted.

I went from a teenager to age thirty-five overnight it seemed. Having fun was for immature, young people, not me. I went to work at the Furr's cafeteria in Utica Square bussing tables. This was similar to my job scraping plates at the University of Oklahoma. The only difference was that the Furr's cafeteria only held maybe a hundred people. There weren't thousands of plates to be scraped like at OU; nevertheless, I stayed busy all the time. I had to wear a white uniform dress, which they provided and ugly white shoes that I had to buy. The shoes, and standing all day, hurt my feet for hours after I came home at night. The worst part was, I was afraid to work. I thought that I might have another *heart attack* while I was at work if I over-exerted myself. I still had no idea that I was suffering from panic attacks.

I also attempted to take classes at Tulsa Junior College so Mama wouldn't feel so bad about me quitting OU to take care of her. I had no major in mind. There was nothing in their catalogue that interested me so I took a pin, let the book fall open and stabbed the pin inside. Computer programming was my new major. I'd never used a computer in my life! Needless to say, this was the wrong way to pick a major. It wouldn't have mattered what the catalogue had opened to, I still wasn't ready to apply myself to academic pursuits. My mind was going a zillion miles a minute. I had tons of more pressing items to think about than political science, English composition, human anatomy and speech. I had to worry about how we were going to survive! To complicate matters, I still desperately wanted to be a nineteen-year-old kid. On a rare occasion, when I did go out with friends, Mama lectured me to no end before I left and also when I returned.

In those days there were no caregiver support groups, at least not to my knowledge. If there was such a group I would have been totally out of place anyway. Most people don't become caregivers to their parents until they are around sixty years old. There was no counseling available for bereavement in the loss of my father. If there was, no one told me about it. There was no social worker, pastor, psychologist or psychiatrist to step in and help me cope with the stress of having a terminally ill mother. I was too naïve to realize she was incurable. I still thought she could get better. I had no close relative or adult to confide in and give me guidance. I needed mental health services and a mentor at the very least. I needed an advocate, a foster parent, anything. At the time, I didn't even know that I needed these things. I was doing the best I could just trying to stay alive. I needed a helping hand. I received no help or services.

My mother had terminal cancer and would be dead by the time I was twenty. My mother had developed lymphoma when I was only twelve. This year marked the beginning of the end of my normal childhood. All I knew was that one night she had a nosebleed that wouldn't stop. She went to the emergency room and they admitted her to the hospital for about a week while they did tests. *How could a nosebleed be that serious?* I wondered. I had never been away from my mother before. I still slept in the same bed with her. I was scared.

I wasn't aware that lymphoma was a type of cancer back then. That's probably a good thing. I would have been terrified if anyone would have told me my mother had cancer. Cancer was a death sentence and *everyone* knew that! I overheard one of the first doctor's she went to say, "In eight years you'll never know that you had this." I guess he was being overly optimistic for my sake, but also very correct. In eight years she would be dead and the dead know nothing. Over the years, we lived as ordinary of a life as possible, in between countless doctors visits. She never had any of the ill effects from chemotherapy to my knowledge. She never lost her hair or threw up. As a matter of fact, her hair, which had started to thin and turn gray, became thick and midnight black with the chemo. I was too young to fully understand what was happening.

On a nice summer day in July, 1984, I was with my mother and Christina, my sister from Arkansas, at the hospital. Our mother was there for another routine chemotherapy treatment. She had been getting treatments like this for years. We would be home in an hour or two. I was sitting in a chair looking at a magazine when I heard, "CODE BLUE," announced on the intercom. I knew what code blue meant. Barbara and Catherine were both nurses and Christina was married to a doctor. I saw the nurses and doctors run into the room my mother was in with a crash cart. She had had a heart attack. They were able to get her heart started again, but now she was in a coma. The doctor apologized that he had never asked my mother what she would prefer in such a situation. What he meant was he had never asked her if she would want to be resuscitated. *Of course, she would want to live!* I screamed silently.

Now, in a coma, it was up to us, her children, to decide her fate. I was twenty. I was officially still a minor until I turned twenty-one. I couldn't be asked to decide if she lived or died if her heart failed again. I looked to Christina and Catherine. They were both in their thirties. They were adults. I'd go along with whatever they said. I'm sure there was the usual discussion about prolonging her life with machines, the suffering she had already endured, the suffering she would have yet to endure, and maybe even something about brain death. I can't remember. My sisters decided that if she had another heart attack that she should not be revived. I was frightened by the thought of this. Everything inside me wanted to argue their decision, but I said nothing. I didn't want to be left totally alone, without a father and a mother!

My mother was hooked up to millions of wires in the intensive care unit. The whole ICU glowed with a bluish light. It was eerie. I asked if anyone ever walks out of ICU. I was told that it does happen. There was a young kid that was involved in a skiing accident and he woke up one day and was fine. Part of me hoped that she would wake up. Maybe she wouldn't have another heart attack and everything would be okay. Part of me knew this was the end. My mother already looked dead and I said so out loud. Barbara told me that, "She can hear you say that. Say something and then look at the monitors."

What do you say to a dead person? I wondered. This isn't natural. It seemed asinine.

I don't know if I spoke or Barbara said something, but sure enough the monitors started jumping around. It was too creepy. She could hear us! I was immediately sorry that I had said she looked dead.

I can remember the paralyzing call from the hospital when my father died. I can even recall what I was doing when I heard that Elvis Presley had died. I was thirteen when Elvis died. I had been riding my bicycle around the rain dampened parking lot of the church down the street from my house; however, I'm not sure where I was, what I was doing, or who told me my mother passed away. On July 11, 1984, Maria Teresa Bassinger was dead at the age of 59.

Almost immediately, I felt a sudden sense of relief. I was free! I could go out with my friends, stay out all night long if I wanted to, and *finally* go on dates. I didn't have to come home in the afternoon to check on her anymore. I didn't have to make sure I laid out something for her to eat while I was gone. There would not be anymore long, boring doctor visits. I'd only have to do my own laundry and clean up my own messes. I'd never have to rinse out her potty stool again. A million other liberating facts raced through my mind. I decided to make up for lost time and indulge myself in every sort of amusement. As quickly as I had had this rush of relief, I felt guilty. What was more important, my fun, freedom, and regained youth, or the fact that she had died? I was being totally selfish.

Almost as quickly as I had felt relief, I felt very frightened. I no longer had a home to go to. It was now up to me to pay all the bills, all the time. If I couldn't, I would die. It was as simple as that. Life itself hung precariously by a thin thread called income. If I couldn't pay for food I would go hungry. If I couldn't afford the gas bill I would freeze. If I couldn't afford to pay rent I would be homeless.

I remembered the mock budget exercise I had done in my high school English class. Mrs. Tibbs had given each of us a pretend salary and a newspaper. With our pay we were to find an affordable apartment, factor in water, electric, phone, and gas bills. We had to buy a car, insurance, food and other things too. My minimum wage salary hadn't even covered the basics. Now the game was real. My future was a menacing void.

A few days after my mother died I had another anxiety attack. I was shaking all over as if I were freezing, but it was summer! Christina was still in town so I asked her to take me to the emergency room. I asked Christina that if I went into a coma that they basically wouldn't cut off my life support. Now, since I knew that young people sometimes recover from the intensive care unit, I didn't want my sisters to terminate my life before I was given every chance possible. Unbelievably, we were both joking and laughing about different things while we were at the emergency room. The doctor looked at us and could see that this was inappropriate behavior for two people who had just lost their mother. He said something about stress being the reason behind why we were laughing. He never once mentioned panic attacks, recommended counseling, or help of any kind. I left the emergency room not knowing why I had had *the shakes*. In my mind, I had decided that I must have some heart defect that the doctors were missing.

Not only did my mother die that day in July, but also, this would be one of the last times I would ever see my sisters. Without any parents, we didn't have any reason to get together. Christina was married to a doctor and had three kids to raise. Catherine had been married since I was two years old and was busy with her career as a nurse. Her husband, Larry, worked doing drafting. They had no children, but they raised about seventy goats out in their country home near Inola, Oklahoma. Barbara was a few days away from turning 27 years old and was single. I had hoped to live in my mother's house for at least a couple of years so I could get an associate's degree of some kind. The house was paid in full and all I would have had to do was pay the monthly utility bills and buy groceries. I could get a part time job and a roommate and I'd be set.

Christina was the *executor of the estate*. Catherine and Christina had decided to sell the house and split the money four ways. After all the funeral expenses and medical bills were paid, we'd each be left with about $3,000. I wouldn't see any of this money for around two years. I had no education, no job, no money, no man in my life, and soon would have nowhere to live. My father had no living relatives that I was aware of except for an elderly cousin that lived in Nowata, Oklahoma, whom I had met only once. My mother had a large family in New York and in Puerto Rico, but I didn't know any of them. I was on my own, alone in the world.

I was an orphan, but I didn't see it that way. Orphans were little kids that lived in group homes, like in the movie, *Little Orphan Annie*. I was too old to be an orphan. Besides, God was my father now. In fact, I remember telling God, "It's just you and me now."

"The helpless commits himself to You; You are the helper of the fatherless," Psalm 10:14, NKJV. I got my things together as quickly as I could and planned to move. Why wait around to be thrown out on the streets? I couldn't delay the inevitable.

I met Jon in September at Eastwood Baptist Church in Tulsa. Before we met, Jon had been working for Standard Oil of Indiana, based in Tulsa, as a computer programmer. Standard Oil laid him off and now he was working with Hudson Consulting as a programmer. Unbelievably, about three months after Hudson hired him they decided to lay him off as well. Luck would have it that Standard Oil of Ohio in Dallas was ready to hire him. Jon had interviewed in Dallas right after Standard Oil of Indiana in Tulsa had let him go.

We didn't realize it when we met, but by December Jon would be moving to Dallas.

Jon still had another month paid up on his apartment on the eastside of town so I moved in when he moved out. I soon discovered that there was no way I could pay for the two bedroom apartment on my own, so after one month I had to move again. I moved into the unfinished attic of my best friend's, mother's house. Christy said that her brothers used to use the attic as their bedroom. It was extremely cold in that attic! The thermometer on the wall read a chilling forty-something degrees in the mornings. It's just a hunch, but I think I know why Randy and Jimmy slept downstairs. I paid her mom for a month's rent and then I was more or less penniless. Even though Christy said that her mom wouldn't throw me out, I wasn't about to stay anywhere that I couldn't pay for. I still had pride back in those days. I was currently jobless so I scoured the want ads, but came up with nothing. I could live in my car. I wouldn't have anything to eat. It was winter and I might die from exposure. I literally prayed that God would let me die quickly from hunger. I didn't understand that people don't die quickly from starvation.

I was down to my last ten bucks when I got an interview for a live-in nanny/housekeeper position in Tahlequah, Oklahoma. I was saved! Room, board and a small salary, $100.00, every week would be excellent! I would also have a "family" again. They had five children ranging from one to thirteen years old. I drove up to Tahlequah and interviewed.

They had the biggest house I had ever seen in my life! My new employers had flown to Dallas, Texas, to get the blueprints for the house on the television series, *Dallas*. Their home was a replica of that house. It was two stories, white, with big columns on the front porch, an in-ground swimming pool and cabana in the backyard, formal dining room, two living areas, kitchen, master bedroom, garage and one and a half baths downstairs. They had a yardman to cut their grass, look after their horses and clean their pool. Upstairs were five bedrooms, a toy room and two full baths. I was to move into the toy room. This was going to take some getting used to for a girl from the west side of Tulsa. I adapted quickly.

All the time that I was living with this family, Jon and I had a long distance relationship. He was in Dallas, Texas and I was in Tahlequah, Oklahoma. I spent most of my $100.00 pay I earned each week on telephone bills. We'd sometimes drive to meet each other on the weekends. We were talking about getting married, but he still hadn't bought an engagement ring for me. Without that ring I still considered myself a free woman. I did go out on a few more dates just to make sure that I really wanted Jon and not someone else. No one else really appealed to me, but I had to keep exploring my options so I could make the best choice. Jon never did buy an engagement ring for me. Wasn't I special enough? This was discouraging and hurtful to me. I was never one of those girls who looked at bridal magazines or dreamed of weddings. In fact, I never even imagined myself as being married. Yet, if we were going to be married I felt like I deserved an engagement ring. Later on, Jon said he didn't think it was important. Not important!? At least he bought a wedding ring. There was no diamond on it though, another disappointment. I had one of the diamonds from my mother's wedding ring placed on my wedding band by a jeweler in Tahlequah.

We were married on November 29, 1985, in the home of his parents in Big Spring, Texas. The only relative I had that came to my wedding was Catherine. However, all the family that I lived with in Tahlequah was there. The youngest girl did my hair for the wedding. She was only eight years old and her mother probably thought I was stupid or something for letting her do my hair. Looking back, maybe I should have had my hair done by a pro, but I liked how she did my hair. Why waste money getting my hair done? The youngest girl also lit the candles that Jon's mother had placed in the living room. The oldest girl, 13 years old, and the second oldest girl, 11 years old, were my bridesmaids. The oldest boy, aged 6, was my ring bearer. The baby boy was too little, so I didn't have a job for him to do at my wedding other than to look cute. I didn't have a father to give me away so I asked the man of the house to do the honors. If I "belonged" to anyone it must be him, he was my employer in any case.

I wore a bridal gown with a hoop skirt and shoes that I had ordered from a J.C. Penney's catalogue. When the shoes arrived they were a little tight, but I kept them anyway. It would have been too much of a hassle to send them back. The dress fit fine. I wasn't much on shopping. The girls all wore dresses that they chose. I couldn't pay for their dresses because I didn't have the money to do so. Therefore, I told them they could wear anything they wanted. I didn't feel entitled to make suggestions or comments on their choice of apparel since I couldn't pay for anything, but I almost died when they wanted to buy business suits! I had imagined something more frilly and elegant. I would have to go along with whatever they decided though. I prayed to God that He wouldn't let them pick those suits. Fortunately enough, the oldest girl decided to wear a white, lace dress and the second oldest girl picked a matching dress. The youngest girl wore a maroon, pageant-style dress. The two little boys wore gray suits. The colors for my wedding had turned out to be maroon, gray and pink. Maroon was in style at the time so it worked out. I still secretly wished that I could have picked my own colors. I wonder what colors I would have chosen?

After the brief ceremony, we went into the dining room for cake and punch. I had told Fran that I wanted a chocolate wedding cake. I was going to buy it myself, but she had insisted that she would buy the cake. I told her, "If you really want to, I guess you can buy it, but make sure it is chocolate."

Much to my disappointment I saw a white wedding cake. This isn't what I wanted at all! I had wanted to be different. I had wanted a chocolate wedding cake with chocolate icing! Fran said, "There's a chocolate groom's cake," as if some small, rather ordinary chocolate cake that looked like it came from a box mix would make things all right. I smiled and pretended that everything was fine. I thought weddings were supposed to be all about the bride. I was so let down.

I brought my best friend's little girl, Krystle, aged 3, with me as my flower girl. Christy, her mom, couldn't make it to the wedding. I didn't mind babysitting Krystle at all. In fact, I enjoyed it immensely. Jon's relatives thought it was stupid to be taking care of a three year old when you're getting married. It isn't like we were going on a honeymoon anywhere. Jon had never mentioned that we would go anywhere. This was also disheartening, but I knew that Jon was once again unemployed at the moment. Standard Oil of Ohio, in Dallas, had laid him off a few weeks before the wedding. Catherine quipped, "At least you could have married someone with a job." I was offended by that remark. It wasn't like Jon was being lazy. He hadn't been fired or quit. He just got laid off again, for the third time. However, from past experiences, I knew better than to openly disagree with Catherine. She'd only make me feel like a stupid little kid.

Jon's sister, Rhonda, insisted that Jon and I at least go to a local hotel for the night and they could take care of Krystle. I hadn't planned on staying anywhere, but in his parent's home that evening. Why should we waste money on a hotel when he didn't have a job? I had no intentions of having wild sex in their house if that is what they were worried about. I wasn't an animal. I could restrain myself. We wound up going to a motel.

The next day we drove back to Dallas with Krystle and Billy Lane, a friend of ours from Tulsa, who had also been at the wedding. We had no heat in the car and it was bitterly cold. All of us stayed in Jon's apartment. The next day I drove back to Oklahoma with Krystle and Billy. I took them home to Tulsa and I drove on to Tahlequah. I told the family I worked for that I would stay with them for another month so they could find someone to take my place. They were surprised that I had come back at all.

One month later I moved in with Jon. I immediately started babysitting for upwardly mobile, very affluent, young couples in the North Dallas and Plano areas. I reasoned with Jon that *any* job was better than no job at all so Jon started working at a Pizza Hut as a delivery driver. Pizza Hut wasn't exactly computer programming, but it was *something* until he could find another professional job.

I suppose we were poor when we were first married, but I hadn't known anything else in my whole life other than being poor. To me everything was normal. In my opinion we were doing fine. We could buy groceries, pay our bills and we weren't on any government assistance. My parents had never accepted any help from the government although they had been eligible for all kinds of assistance, I'm sure. Begging for help from the government or from anyone for that matter was a sign of failure in my family. Adults stood on their on feet. Adults worked and paid their own way. Jon didn't think we were doing okay, but he kept it to himself for the most part. He hadn't known anything, but being well off all his life.

Let me digress. When Jon and I were first married, I heard an incredible story. Jon's sister, Lisa, was married to a college professor. Word has it that her husband's father was a self-made millionaire by way of driving a taxi cab. Now, I'm not exactly sure how a cabbie becomes a millionaire, but apparently Lisa's father in-law had pulled it off. I found this to be amazing and applaudable and I said so! Jon's mother was quick to reply that, "It doesn't take a lot to be a millionaire anymore."

I wasn't sure how to take that statement. I felt like I had been slapped in the face. I must be stupid and have a poverty mentality that prevented me from seeing how easy it was to make a million dollars. I was almost embarrassed. I had never really considered what little a million could probably buy. I had always considered how *much* such a large amount could buy. Maybe a million dollars couldn't buy what it used to. Maybe it really was easy to make a million. Maybe people had to be billionaires to be considered rich now. A million bucks still sounded like an unreal amount of money to me.

Eleven months after we were married, Sara Anne Riley came into the world on October 18, 1986. Neither of us had health insurance. Sara didn't have insurance either. This really didn't bother me. My parents had never carried insurance on any of my siblings or myself when we were growing up either. Insurance was unaffordable. If Medicaid existed back then, or was available to us, I had no idea. I learned that hospitals really don't like to mess with people without insurance. When I was a few weeks away from delivering, the hospital told me that I wouldn't be allowed to give birth there because they weren't a charity hospital. My obstetrician didn't work at the charity hospital! I didn't know what to do. I didn't want charity. I told them I would pay out of pocket for the birth. I had completely paid off all my doctor's bills during the nine months I had been pregnant and I told the hospital as much. I said I'd have to pay them over time. They didn't believe me of course, nor did they care. They wanted the money up front or I wouldn't be allowed in the hospital when the time came. When I went back to the hospital to have the baby I told Jon to just lie and tell them we had insurance. I told him we could deal with them when I checked out. It took us until Sara's second birthday to pay off the hospital bill from when she was born. It was by the grace of God that we stayed healthy during the next two years without insurance. I had not yet acquired asthma or diabetes and the pregnancy and birth were without complications.

At the young age of two weeks old, Sara started going to work with me. I was still babysitting for wealthy, North Dallas couples at the time. However, I would soon start work at The Good News Christian Daycare. I didn't necessarily see it as my life's ambition to work in daycare, but it was the only option I had available to me at the time. Besides, daycare work was fulfilling to me. I was a young mother. My main interest was my baby, in particular, and anything having to do with babies, in general. I felt I was becoming quite the expert on young children. The work made me feel important. Jon's mother insisted that I just liked children and I *wanted* to work in these low paying daycare centers. Fran suggested that I should go out and find a job that paid at least $10.00 an hour. I should have known right then that his overly affluent mom was completely out of touch with anyone who wasn't of her same social status. It is now twenty years later, 2006, and most people where I live, in Central Illinois, still do not make $10.00 an hour.

Anyway, most daycare facilities in the 1980s offered their workers free or cheap childcare. If I worked anywhere else I would have had to pay full price for daycare. In that case, it wouldn't have been worth it to go to work because, quite literally, all my earnings would be going to daycare costs. I wasn't educated or trained to do anything that would have paid me enough to afford the cost of daycare and still have a decent amount of paycheck leftover to live on. Jon's mother always hated it when I said I wasn't educated and she told me not to say that. I know that now there are assistance programs to help pay for daycare, but I was not aware of any such programs in 1986. I doubt they existed then.

On Sara's second birthday, Jon was hired by LTV Aircraft in Dallas. I had filled out the job application for him and sent it in. I had no idea if I was filling the application out correctly or not. I wasn't familiar with all the computer terms on his resume, but the application had been on his desk at home for months. Jon was horrible about filling out applications or acting on job leads. He'd circle ads in the newspaper and never call, pick up an application or send in a resume. I couldn't understand why he bought the newspaper if he didn't intend to go see about the job. Even this bizarre behavior didn't really bother me too much, not yet anyway.

We moved to the Dallas area, Grand Prairie to be exact, and began our life as a young, middle-class, family. This was the first time in my life that I had not been officially poor. It was great. I quit work and became a stay-at-home mom. I felt rich.

On November 1, 1989, Jon Daniell Riley was born. He had the exact same name as Big Jon. I didn't want any "Junior" or "the second" added to his name. Instead, I insisted on calling him "Little Jon" from the start. The name Daniell was spelled with two "L's" as Big Jon's middle name had been spelled. Daniell was Jon's maternal grandfather's last name, Forest Daniell.

This time we had insurance. Things were much nicer with insurance. Things were better in every way possible. We were living in a rental house for the first time, not a cramped apartment. We had a dog. I had always wanted a dog when I was growing up and had not been allowed to have one. We had a fenced backyard for the kids to play in. The homeowner's even let me dig up a small garden.

About a year after Little Jon was born we bought our first house! I never dreamed I'd have my own house. Life was good. We had also found a good church and made new friends. My kids were spoiled. I bought all sorts of toys for them. I took them everywhere with me. I rarely had a babysitter. I enjoyed dressing them up like brother and sister twins. We went to parks, the zoo, museums and all sorts of places that I thought were educational and that they might like. Almost everything I did centered around the kids.

The job at LTV lasted for four, wonderful, stress-free years. I should have known it was too good to last. Jon got laid off. He started working as a contract programmer almost immediately. He'd work for a few months with one company and then a few months with another company. Still, I didn't have a problem with this. Our life was still very good. When Jon had work he brought home good money. It was a little scary waiting for the next job to come along though. The "temp for hire" life took us to Springfield, Illinois for six months, then to Kansas City for fourteen months, then back to Springfield. Toward the end of our second "tour of duty" in Springfield we bought our country home that we live in today. Seemingly, as soon as we had the papers on the house signed, Jon lost his career altogether for sleeping on the job.

Chapter Three:
The Not So Carefree College Years

Fifteen years after my high school graduation, I desperately needed the college degree that was denied me when I was younger. It was always my plan to be a music teacher. I couldn't even drive by a university without wanting to cry in regret for what could have been mine if only my parents had lived longer. I avoided listening to others talk about college, careers and graduations. I was jealous, sad and felt like I didn't belong around other adults that had their degrees. I felt as if I had let my parents down by not getting my degree. There was no way I could afford to pay for an education. No matter, it had to be done. My husband had abandoned his position, willingly or unwillingly, as breadwinner. I had to take action. I enrolled at Millikin University, in Decatur, Illinois, as a music education major. In four years time I would be able to get a job that would support my family.

Jon had just received half of a sixty thousand dollar inheritance from his deceased grandmother, Florence Riley. We would use this money to live on while I was in school. Sixty thousand dollars seemed like a lot of money, but if you divided that by the four and a half years I was in school, it came to slightly more than $13,000 per year to live on. Thirteen thousand dollars a year for a family of four is destitution. Jon told me that his Dad, Dr. William A. Riley, had offered to pay my way through college when we were first married. Why hadn't I heard of this offer?! This was great! As poor as we were, I could get the maximum amount in federal student aid grants from the government. I'd get a small music scholarship too. Jon's mom could just pick up what was left. If it were only this easy.

Jon's parent's had paid for their son-in-law to go to medical school. This particular son-in-law had supposedly cheated on Jon's sister with some of the nursing staff at the medical facility he worked at. Allegedly, he got hooked on prescription drugs and lost his medical license because of it. For the Grand Finale, he left Jon's sister when she was pregnant with their third child. Of course, that may not be the exact order in which things happened, but nevertheless, that is the basic rundown of the gossip. I'm not privy to all the facts because I never asked and really don't care. I figured I'd keep my young impressionable kids away from their soap opera. Thankfully, Dr. Riley died before the crap hit the fan.

Surely, whatever the truth was, the actions of the ex-son-in-law made me the "good" in-law. I hadn't cheated on Jon, abandoned my children *or* been addicted to drugs. Heck, I didn't even smoke, drink or curse. I didn't even drink coffee! The cussing and the coffee would come later, but for now, I was totally blameless. Certainly, Fran would still make good on Dr. Riley's offer to pay my way through college.

However, Jon's mom sounded as if college wasn't the right thing for me. She preferred that I just get a job. Well, yeah, duh, that's why I was going to college. I don't think Fran understood that unless you have a college education you are pretty much cast into working for minimum wage the rest of your life.

Fran was positive I didn't need an education to be successful. She said, "Leah, you're so smart." She told me that her sister, or someone, had taught school without a college degree during the war. They had been desperate for teachers, or so she said. Excuse me? The war? What war? World War II was over fifty years ago! Things were probably a little bit different back then. In 1997, you don't teach anywhere unless you have the piece of paper from a university to say you are qualified! Being "smart" is inconsequential. I could apply for a job as a brain surgeon and tell them how "smart" I was, but they'd want to see the papers.

Jon's mother insisted that Bill Gates, of Microsoft fame, never went to college. Did I look like a computer genius to her?! Right…

She suggested that I could sell used cars. Apparently, someone she knew or some infomercial she had seen made her believe that selling cars was the way to riches. Are you kidding me? I didn't know anything about cars!

Fran was ever persistent. Jon and I could sell mass spectrometers. What? Christian, one of Jon's brothers-in-law, was supposedly making obscene amounts of money selling these things. General rule of thumb, if you have never heard of something before, you probably shouldn't try and sell it. What was a mass spectrometer? What did it do? I'd never heard of one, ever! I found out that it had something to do with math and chemistry. That pretty much shot that idea out the window for me. Math? Computers? Chemistry? She seriously overestimated my talents.

This idea was one of her craziest…she decided that we should all move to Branson and form a family act. We could be like the Osmond family. God help us! I was the only "musician" in the family and I use that word very loosely. I wasn't a singer. I was an instrumentalist. I usually refrained from singing at church. My voice didn't go very high at all. The female parts were way too high for me. I had to constantly keep switching octaves when we sang hymns. My maiden name hadn't been BASSinger for nothing!

Big Jon had a nice singing voice. Big Jon also had no rhythm and could not carry any part other than the melody. However, if someone else started singing harmony, Jon would follow them and drop the melody. Jon couldn't hold his own. Singing in parts is a skill to be sure. I was probably as bad as Jon when it came to singing in parts. I'd really never tried it. On top of that, we didn't have the outgoing personalities or the good looks to be entertainers. This was a really bad idea!

Jon's mom had been a 1950's stay-at-home mom and housewife. She was not in touch with the plight of the working woman of the 1990's. She had no idea what it took to get a decent job. Well-to-do women, such as herself, generally went to college to find a rich man to marry. Maybe, she thought I was going to college to find a rich man so I could dump Jon. Women of her social standing usually weren't interested in a career for themselves. Women of the 1950's certainly didn't go to college with the intent of single-handedly supporting their children and their disabled husbands with their degree. Men, as a rule, were the wage earners. The woman's place was in the home. Fran had gone from having her daddy support her to having her husband support her. She was clueless.

When Fran wasn't trying to tell us what to do she was sending us literature that told us what to do. The many financial books and money management pamphlets Fran sent did not apply to us. I know that Fran did not comprehend what we were going through. I'm sure that it was quite inconceivable to her. The books and pamphlets Fran sent assumed that the reader had a living wage, workable income. The literature also assumed that there was some amount of discretionary income available, a lot of discretionary income in most cases. I mean really, what is a book titled, "Wealth Without Risks", going to do for someone like us? Absolutely nothing is the answer, but yet she sent it to us. What was Jon's mom thinking? Did she believe that we had wads of money stashed away somewhere that we weren't telling her about? I was a broke, soon to be college kid, with no marketable skills and Jon was jobless! She either couldn't or wouldn't accept that fact. Maybe she was simply too inexperienced with the harsher realities of life to understand.

We were the black sheep in Jon's, otherwise affluent, extended family. We must have been an embarrassment to his mother I'm sure. All the other ladies, at her retirement home where she lived, probably had prosperous children that they bragged about continually. Here I was at age thirty-three, just now starting college. I didn't have any investments, savings, or an established career in a good company. Then again, I wasn't her daughter so she could pass the blame for my deficiencies on to someone else. She could live vicariously through one of her other children. Roanne, Lisa and Rhonda were well off. She'd just have to limit her conversations to talking about them and their prosperous husbands.

Fran even quit asking her friends to pray for Jon to find a job. Jon's job situation had gone on for years so, I suppose it was very awkward for her. No mother would want to keep reminding all her friends and associates that her son and his wife are complete and total losers. I guess her Sunday school was tired of hearing about Jon's unending work instability. If they weren't sick of his predicament, then I'm sure it bothered them. After all, if this could happen to one of Fran's children then maybe it could happen to one of their children too! If it happened to one of *their* children then, they might feel obligated to help their own child and we couldn't have that now could we? That would mess up their carefree, golden years of retirement!

Finally, Jon's mother indicated that she would help me and even take a job, if she had to, to see that I got through college. I truly didn't believe that his mother would actually get a job. She was in her sixties, so it was kind of late for her to be deciding to have a career now. I should have known that this meant, "You're on your own", but I was stupid.

I went to the financial aid office at Millikin and received the maximum amount of federal grant money allowable to me. I'd have to pay for the rest of my tuition with student loans. Jon's mother would surely help me pay on the loans. Being in debt wasn't going to be fun, but I could easily pay off my loans with the job I would get after graduation, or so I thought. How idiotically optimistic I was!

It was my first semester back to school in fifteen years and I still felt that I was scholastically substandard. Additionally, I had no idea if I could financially afford to finish all four years. My family needed things. We didn't have a breadwinner. Maybe I had made a mistake. Perhaps, I really couldn't cut it academically. I just wasn't as good as other people. I remembered all those "F's" on my previous college transcripts. Millikin immediately put me on academic probation. I over studied that first semester and pulled off straight A's! I wasn't second-rate at all. If anything I was going to be just fine. My brain wasn't impaired. I wasn't deficient in the slightest. I had just been under too much stress when I had been at the University of Oklahoma. No one could have been expected to concentrate on their studies under such conditions as I had back then. My confidence was back. My dream of a college education was on its way to being fulfilled, at least for now.

With Jon not working, or barely working the whole time I was in school, we had little money. I was unable to work due to the heavy course load I had to take in order to graduate on time before the financial aid ran out. One semester, I was taking twenty-six credit hours which, amounted to ten real-time hours in class on some days. That doesn't take into consideration that I still had to study for these classes and try to squeeze in a little time for my kids.

Jon was not keeping the house while I was gone all day and all night at Millikin. Call it depression, call it laziness on his part, it doesn't matter. My house was not being cleaned and I had no time to do anything about it. I sure could have used one of his family's maids about right now. "Dream on Cinderlea," I told myself. Cinderlea, a derivative of Cinderella and Leah, was a name my mother used to call me sometimes. In the story, Cinderella was a poor maid to her evil stepfamily. I had been a maid once when I lived in Tahlequah. I could guarantee that I would probably never have such a luxury.

I found out later what had occupied all of Jon's free time. We frequently rented videotapes from Family Video to watch at home. We had several to return so Jon suggested that I take them back. This wasn't a problem. I made sure they were all rewound and searched around the living room to find all their outer plastic cases. One video in particular shocked me. It was a porn movie. I certainly hadn't rented this! The kids were too young to even know what pornography was. Little Jon was only seven and Sara was ten. I held the video in my hands for several minutes. I was terrified for some reason. I didn't confront Jon about it at the time. I was that frightened! I wasn't afraid of Jon, I was scared of what this meant. What did this mean? I supposed that it was a mistake. Maybe it wasn't really his. I don't know what I was thinking. I hoped it would all go away.

This problem didn't resurface its ugly head again for at least a couple of years. The next time I was aware of Jon's addiction to pornography came when Sara discovered a page of a nudie magazine tucked under the front seat of the car. We had been cleaning out the car. This time I confronted him. He said he had hid the rest of the magazine out in the woods behind our house. According to Jon, I was to blame for his new hobby. I supposedly never had time for him anymore. I didn't have time for a lot of things anymore. Sleep was one of those things. Did he really think I was going to give up the two to six hours of sleep I did get, to have sex?! Maybe he would prefer that I cut classes, not study for a test, or give up symphony practices in order to have time for sex. During one particular Christmas break from Millikin, I came home and slept for seventeen hours straight. I did this for three days in a row. I was that tired! Jon was being totally unreasonable.

As the sleep deprivation built up, I demonstrated some really bizarre behaviors. One day I drove over to a Hardees to buy a burger. I went through the drive-through lane. I sat and waited for several minutes. Where was the employee? When were they going to ask for my order? They sure were taking a long time. I sat patiently. Finally, I came out of my trance and realized I was parked beside the newspaper box not the ordering screen.

Another time, I was in a lane of traffic outside the music building. A large group of fraternity guys were excitedly waiting to cross the street. I motioned them across. It was cold and dark outside. Why were they wearing only summer shorts and no shirts? Whatever, I didn't care. I just wanted the last of them to cross the street so I could park and get to orchestra rehearsal. One of the guys stopped in front of my car, banged on the hood and did a little dance. Oh, okay, I get it. I smiled. The must be practicing for the *bun run*, a tradition at Millikin. The first snowfall after the second semester started was the official date for the run each year. The frat boys would streak across campus and run butt-naked through a few buildings including the girl's dorm. Those weren't summer shorts they were wearing this evening, those were boxers! I was supposed to have been impressed. Now I felt bad. They were putting on a show for me and I hadn't even clapped for them. I had been too tired to even know what was going on much less be impressed by their display of male physique.

For several months I didn't find any more evidence of porn in my car or home. Jon must have repented. After all, he was a Christian. You repent and move on. Not in this case. My next encounter with Jon's pastime was quite interesting. I had, by now, learned how to check the history on my computer at home. Jon had a very active pornographic record on the computer. I pulled up one of the websites Jon had been visiting. I could make out naked body parts, but I wasn't sure what I was looking at. It was a tangle of legs and genitalia. Whose legs were whose? What was happening in this picture? I couldn't quite decide. It was almost like looking at one of those optical illusion puzzles. First you see one picture then it turns into another picture. After several minutes of studying this image I realized I was looking at two males. Two males! Oh my God!

Now, I was enraged! I knew I had to be more appealing than that! I told him if that is what he wanted he could have it, but he wasn't going to touch me. He swore he hadn't been looking at the gay porn, only the redheaded females. So he had a redhead fetish. This was a good thing I thought, in some small, sick and twisted way, seeing as I was a redhead. Still, if he wanted to lust after those flat-chested redheaded sluts on the net, he wasn't having me. He insisted that he wanted me, not those whores, but I never reciprocated his advances. Had he considered showering? His hygiene level had fallen to an all time low. Had he considered how tired I was? I was in college! I had to get an education so we could live! Had he considered how I resented him for leaving me high and dry to support the family on my own? I was stressed and running scared. I was scared that I wouldn't be able to get enough loans and grants to finish my education. If I didn't graduate we'd never be able to survive! He wanted sex?! How selfish and immature! I had enough to worry about without this bullcrap!

This is how Jon respected me?! I was incensed! There I was trying to get an education so I could support his butt and this is what he does to me?! He was lusting after other women. Small-breasted women at that! In my Bible it says somewhere that to lust after a porn whore with small tits is the same as committing adultery with her. Jon had, in essence, cheated on me. This was Biblical grounds for divorce. I can't say the thought hadn't crossed my mind, but Jon and the kids were my only family. What's more, I couldn't even afford the small fee for a cheapo divorce. Besides, I didn't want to start over now. We probably should have been in marriage counseling, but I seriously didn't have the money or the time for that either.

Due to our constant financial strain we had several problems. The car had its difficulties. Every time we wanted to start the car we had to get a jump. We borrowed a battery charger from one of our neighbors for a week or two. Then, we borrowed another charger from a different neighbor for an additional few weeks. All this was just to be able to get the car to start in the mornings. Whenever we went somewhere, someone had to stay in the car and keep it running so we wouldn't have to hail down some stranger to jump us. Sometimes, if Jon or I were by ourselves, if we gunned the engine up for a few minutes before we turned the car off it might start again without a jump. Finally, after about two months we managed to scrounge up the money to get the car fixed.

Just when I thought Millikin might be a place to get away from the ever-present doom of home life, Jesse Jackson appears. That's right, *the* Jesse Jackson. Sometime in September of 1999, seven students that attended Decatur public schools got in a fight. They got their butts expelled and sent to an alternative school. Nothing wrong so far you say? Well, these students just happened to be black and Reverend Jackson had to come down and make everything into a racial war. The punishment was too harsh supposedly. Personally, the way schools are going down the toilets these days, I don't think punishments are harsh enough! When I was in school you could hear the crack of those wooden paddles they made in shop class echoing in the halls at least once a day. Red, yellow, black or white, it didn't matter. No one would be driving across the country to intercede for your blistered buttocks! You got what you deserved. Funny thing is, by the time most kids got to high school they no longer needed *whoopins*, as we called them, because they had learned how to act. Imagine.

So anyway, little ol' me goes over to the closest high school to Millikin. I had to put in my observation hours for student teaching. I found my way blocked by security guards at the door. They were not about to let me in without being interrogated. The schools were on lock down. I resented the fact that I should be questioned like a criminal because some punk high school kids don't know how to behave. I snuck around the back, found an unguarded door, and let myself into the orchestra room to observe the class. I had to do what I had to do. I needed to turn these notes in for a grade. Hell, high water, and even the Reverend Jackson were not going to keep me from my assignment. I was paying too much for these Milli-classes to flunk out and have to take the class again.

I was learning one thing. When Jesse comes to town, trouble usually follows. Reverend Jackson successfully rallied a significant number of the black community of Decatur into an emotional frenzy. I had a guess of what might happen next. I figured that every wannabe white supremacist would crawl out of the woodwork, shave their heads, don their military/biker/gothic looking clothes, maybe wave a rebel flag around and cause problems. There might even be violence.

Well I was wrong. The skinhead, Neo-Nazis, whatever they are, never showed up, to my knowledge. Thank God for that you say? Well, what *did* appeared on the scene scared the living crap out of me. I could have lived with some young, angry, skinheads making fools out of themselves. I wasn't prepared for what I saw.

The news crews were out in force. The Ku Klux Klan was coming!! Holy God! The KKK really exists?! I thought that stuff was ancient history. I mean, I had seen old documentaries once in awhile on the Public Broadcasting Station about the Ku Klux Klan. You gotta be kidding me! I was scared. Now, exactly *why* I was scared I don't really know. For all practical purposes I was as Caucasian as the next white person. The KKK weren't going to hang me, burn a cross in my yard or whatever it is they do. *I hoped.*

Nevertheless, I was still nervous, but curious at the same time. I had to see this oddity, grown men, wearing bed sheets, rallying at the park, in broad daylight. It was unbelievable. I couldn't help myself. I drove to the park. I was still kind of wondering if I would be shot at or something. How violent were these guys nowadays? Did they still hang people from trees like in the documentaries on television? Would they somehow magically know I was half Hispanic on my mother's side of the family? They hate Hispanics don't they? I cruised around. Then I saw them. Oh my God! This wasn't television. There they were, in the flesh! I must have been gawking at them like I had just seen an alien spaceship land. Now, I know it's impolite to stare, but this was a once in a lifetime event. I should have brought a camera. There didn't seem to be many of them. It sort of looked like they were either just arriving or had recently finished their meeting. Man! I had wanted to hear what they would say. I thought all their robes would be white. Some of them had on different colors. Who were these guys? Were they locals? I hoped they weren't anyone I knew. I couldn't see their faces, but they could see mine. What if they thought that my presence there meant I supported this kind of thing? I stayed in my car.

It was unreal. I wondered if I knew any of the people under those robes. How embarrassing that would be. We were in Illinois. I thought the Ku Klux Klan was strictly a southern thing. How far did these guys drive to get here? I should have thought to bring a camera. Racism seemed to be alive and well in Decatur. Now, if I could just get home without having Jesse and his mob on one side of the street and the Klan on the other side of the street I would be fine. You would have thought this was 1899 not 1999.

Unfortunately, this Jesse verses the Klan was not the only time I'd see blatant racism in Illinois. Call me sheltered, but until this point in my life I hadn't really seen much racism. When we first moved to Illinois and were looking for a place to live a real estate lady had told me, "You don't want to live there. That's were all the blacks live." I was taken aback by this. How unprofessional was *that*? I had never heard anyone say things like that in a work atmosphere before. Sure, I'd heard people say all kinds of things when they weren't working, but this was so uncalled for. How did she know for a fact I wasn't black? We were talking on the telephone, after all.

I suppose my first experience with actual hate mongers came when I was part of the Millikin symphony. One of our violinists just happened to be Matt Hale of the World Church of the Creator! Matt Hale came into the limelight following the summer when some of his "disciples" decided to go on a killing spree. Now, Matt never really caused problems at orchestra rehearsals at all, but Millikin put two and two together and promptly threw him out of the orchestra. This was the right thing to do I suppose, but I was concerned that Matt Hale might retaliate. I was afraid to go to orchestra practice and concerts. We had a Jewish conductor and a handful of persons of color in the symphony. My chair in the symphony was almost directly in front of the conductor. I hoped to God that if Matt, or his band of followers, decided to kill the conductor in retaliation, that they didn't miss and accidentally shoot me instead. I really didn't have anything against the director, I just wanted to live you know?

During the first two years that I was at Millikin we had enrolled the kids at Northwest Christian Campus in Decatur. Now, we could no longer afford to send them to a private school. Besides, Little Jon needed special education for dyslexia. Special education services are usually not offered at most private schools. Big Jon hadn't helped matters. He had acted irresponsibly and not helped Little Jon with his homework while he was enrolled at Northwest Christian. In fact, Big Jon never even told Little Jon to do his homework at all, according to Sara. I was never home due to my own heavy course schedule. Even when I *was* home I wasn't really there. I was forever either writing a paper or studying. Little Jon was subsequently left behind a grade. Little Jon would have to repeat third grade again next year.

Little Jon was ten and Sara was thirteen when they started attending the Taylorville Public Schools. Still, I was worried about sending them to a public school. First, I wanted them to stay in a Christian environment. Second, school shootings were becoming more and more frequent. I expressed my concerns to Fran hoping that maybe she would make it possible for her grandchildren to continue in the Christian school. Fran's reply was, "Those are the chances you have to take."

I'm not sure what she meant by that. Jon always said that his mother wasn't one to think before she spoke. I didn't like the sound of it in any case. Sara interpreted Fran's words to mean that her grandmother wanted her to come home from school in a body bag.

Early in the summer of 2000 I was working at Step by Step daycare as a preschool teacher. I felt like I should be at home with my kids, but we needed the money desperately. Little Jon was only eleven and I knew he needed someone to look after him. I couldn't afford a babysitter or a day camp. Sara was at home with him, but Little Jon, more than likely, would be outside in the woods somewhere and Sara would be inside the house all summer. Would she check on him? Could she determine if a situation was an emergency? Little Jon was allergic to insect bites and stings. What if he fell out of a tree and knocked himself unconscious or broke his neck? What if he decided to go near the river? He could swim, but what about undercurrents? It worried me. Anything could happen. Ironically, I had a job taking care of other people's children and I couldn't be there to take care of my own.

Step by Step was only a summer job for me because I was going back to Millikin in the fall. This was a great daycare. My assistant teacher was easy to get along with. The kids were as tame as could be expected for being three and four year olds. We got to go on field trips. The food, which was becoming a scarcity at home, was free here and it tasted pretty good, too.

On an ordinary, summer, day Jon drove by Step by Step. He was bringing me the car on my lunch hour. I would take him to work at Burger King and then drive back to my work. As soon as I went outside I felt a little like throwing up. I surmised that I had eaten one too many chicken fried steak patties for lunch. We started driving across Springfield and I became more nauseous. My body started to tingle in places and I was becoming tired. I'd shake it off. Jon got out of the car at the Burger King and I started driving back.

I didn't make it too far when I felt like I was blacking out. Instead of pulling over, the only thing I could think of was to speed up and get to the hospital. The hospital was right across from where I worked. I thought I was having a diabetic moment. I hadn't been able to buy any test strips in a long time because we were too broke. I had no idea what my sugar levels had been running. I barely made it to the ER. I parked the car and went in. By now, I was hyperventilating. They checked my blood sugar. It was high, but not anything wildly abnormal. They admonished me that I should get some test strips. Test strips cost $40.00. I wish I had that kind of extra money lying around! The doctor asked if there was anyone I could call. Not really. Jon was at work and he didn't have a car to come get me. I puked up my lunch and they gave me a grape Popsicle. After an hour in the emergency room I started to feel normal again. The doctor came in to sign me out.

"Have you been under any stress lately?"

"Well yeah, I'm always under stress, but I'm used to it," I replied.

"Has anything happened today?"

"Well, my electricity and phone got turned off this morning and I don't have any water in my house either because the pump for the well runs on electricity," I suggested. "But this is all normal for me," I insisted. "I wasn't stressing about any of those things. I wasn't even thinking about it. I was just at work doing my job."

"Sometimes you don't have to be thinking about it. When the body has had enough stress placed on it, it will succumb to that stress no matter what your mind set is," he shared.

The doctor hadn't mentioned the words, "panic attack", but I was beginning to believe that this was my problem. The panic attacks were just manifesting themselves differently now than they had twenty years ago. I didn't have the rapid heartbeats and palpitations anymore. Barbara had once told me that, I didn't handle stress very well. I guess she was right.

Later that same summer, in August, I managed to land in St. Vincent's Memorial hospital in Taylorville with abdominal pains. Little Jon had been a patient in this same hospital, not long ago, with severe asthma. He had liked his stay. They fed him well and he got to play video games. I thought Little Jon just had a cold. I gave him some cold medicine, scheduled a doctor's appointment for that afternoon, and left. I learned later that the cold syrup I had given Little Jon had only made his asthma worse. Big Jon stayed home from Burger King to take him to the doctor. The doctor took one look at him and immediately admitted him. If I hadn't been able to make an appointment for that day he might have been dead!

I'm not sure what was wrong with me. I don't think the doctors were sure either. This time it wasn't stress, at least I don't think so. It was some kind of painful, abdominally centered infection. I could barely walk. Lying in bed was painful. At first, the doctor thought I was having appendicitis and intended to operate. I had to go without food for two days while they decided whether to operate or not. After some high-powered, intravenous antibiotics I felt a little better and went home. No food or video games for me.

It was at times like this that I desperately wanted another mother. I had expressed my longing for another set of parents, or at least another mom, to several people. Mostly, I was ridiculed, told to "grow up", or they questioned my motives. I simply missed the caring and nurturing. I had Jon, but he wasn't the nurturing kind.

When we had been newlyweds I had hoped that Jon's parents would consider me as one of their own daughters. They already had four daughters, Karen, Rhonda, Lisa and Roanne. They didn't need another daughter. This became very apparent when Sara and I were left out of their generational photo when she was a baby. The "real" daughters were asked to stand in a picture with their Grandmother Daniell, their mother, and their new babies. Four generations were represented. I had never considered such a photograph. I hadn't really known my own grandmother. I thought this was a great idea. They gleefully smiled and posed. I held Sara and watched. We weren't invited to join. Did they have any idea how much I wanted them to invite us into the picture? That hurt.

About three quarters of the way through my Millikin years we hit the bottom. We had to ask Jon's family for financial help. His mom agreed to give us around $1500 a month for our living expenses for one school year. This was great! However, the conditions placed on this arrangement were less than enviable. If Fran said it once, she said it a gillion times, "He who has the money makes the rules!" Yep, she made the rules all right. Actually, it was one of Jon's brothers in-law that dictated to us what we were to buy and not buy with Fran's money. We were not to buy any prepackaged cereals or cookies. We were also banned from purchasing soda pop and many other items that were deemed unnecessary. The list included junk food of all kinds and most forms of entertainment. I suppose they wanted us to be super healthy and bored. They need not have worried. There isn't a whole lot a family of four can do on $1,500 a month anyway. However, with Fran being in Texas and the brother in-law also out of state, it was hard for them to enforce their stringent rules. I know we bought some pop with her money. She probably could guess that we bought some of these items as well and, in all probability, it infuriated her.

We were told we had to live on a "Spartan" budget. All purchases beyond the $1,500, such as strings for my viola or doctor's bills had to be pre-approved. In other words, Fran and her financial manager, the brother in-law, had to have a receipt for the goods we bought in order to reimburse us. Some items, such as prescription eyeglasses were deemed unnecessary expenses, so I did without. It was next to impossible to pay for something extra up front when we didn't have very much money to begin with. It would have been better for them to send us the money so we could actually buy the item, then we could send them the receipt. They didn't operate like that. I guess they didn't trust us not to buy illegal drugs and liquor or go gambling with the money. You can fill in the blank with whatever money wasting sin you can possibly imagine. Obviously, we had indulged ourselves and not been good *stewards* of our money. Otherwise, we wouldn't be in this position, or so Jon's family must have assumed. I'm pretty sure that they equate poverty with some sin in the life of the one impoverished. If we hadn't committed some unpardonable sin then I imagine we were, at the very least, unintelligent, poor, white, filth that had no idea how to manage money or the value of a dollar. Whatever.

Living at the mercy of others is not fun, but it was necessary. We were totally dependent on Jon's mom and there was nothing I could do about it. I was carrying a huge course load in order to graduate before my financial aid ran out! I had to graduate at any cost, even the cost of being bossed around by the *Money Gestapo*. After about nine months of being told what I could and could not do, I told Jon's family what *they could do!* I'm sure this came as a huge shock to Mr. Brother in-law. He didn't seem like the type that was used to being told off in no uncertain terms. Needless to say, this verbal can of whoop ass that I hurled at him unmistakably ended the cash flow. I was nearing the end of my Milli-career and I could handle it from here on out. At least I'd have enough hours freed up from classes to work somewhere now.

Our phone had been turned off due to non-payment. Having the phone disconnected was the best thing that could have happened to us. By this point, I was actually having dreams at night about grabbing his sister and brother-in-law by the shirt collar, pinning them to a wall and punching them until they apologized to us. Apparently, I had more than two arms in my dream because I had both of them lifted up, about a foot off the ground, one in each hand, and I was still able to fist them square in the face with a third hand.

I was severely depressed. I couldn't handle anything anymore. I took some time off to go to and see if there were any anti-depressant drugs that might help me. I had never been on anti-depressants before, but I was desperate. My family doctor asked me, "Do you feel like hurting yourself?" I looked at him like he was nuts. "I don't want to kill myself," I assured him. "I'd rather kill someone else!"

I think he took that the wrong way. He looked concerned. I didn't mean it like that. I'd never really hurt anyone else unless it was self-defense or in one of my dreams. The doctor urged me to go to the Christian County Mental Health Clinic. I talked to the lady I was assigned to, but she didn't help me. She had no idea what I was going through and over simplified my problems. I saw her once. Talking was pointless. It wasn't going to change my situation. The Celexa that I was prescribed worked wonders though. I didn't feel drugged at all. The medicine made me calm down a lot. I no longer cared what Jon's relatives did or said.

When I was able to get the phone turned on again, a couple of months later, I had the number changed. This one small act did wonders for my sanity. I'm sure it drove his mom crazy because she was no longer in control. She couldn't just pick up the phone and call anymore.

She wasn't at liberty to question our every move or give unwanted input. Since she couldn't call us directly, Fran called the local police in Christian County and had them go to our house to see if we still lived there! We were surprised to see a cop come up our driveway. The policeman told Jon that he should, "Call his mom," and then he left.

While we were under the in-laws complete control, every one of us had been prescribed anti-depressants. Big Jon had been the first to be prescribed anti-depressants. He was on Welbutrin. Sara and Little Jon had been on Zoloft. Now, with the phone number changed, these drugs were not needed as much. After a period of time, I quit taking the Celexa. I also lost the twenty-five pounds that it had made me gain. We didn't give any of Jon's relatives our phone number for almost two years. It was much more peaceful this way. We told them we didn't have a phone. Maybe they believed us and maybe they didn't. Either way, I didn't care.

Does it sound like I am ungrateful? Jon's Mom always thought we were ungrateful. I was very thankful at first for her help. I never would have made it through Millikin had Jon's mother not decided to pick up our living expenses for a year. I would have had to drop out and just grab any job I could find. However, a person can only deal with so much. I didn't really know where their philosophy of, "He who has the money makes all the rules," comes from. I searched for this saying online. The saying apparently originated in Europe somewhere and it was applied to business situations. I will say this. That philosophy stinks when it is applied to personal relationships!

Jon's sister eventually apologized to me in a greeting card she sent. She was determined to have us come to her house for Christmas. She wanted everyone to have family pictures taken with Fran. His sister stated, "We don't know how long she will live."

I figured that I probably wouldn't be invited to join in the picture, especially not now. I told Jon that he could go if he wanted to, but I was way to raw from the whole ordeal. To put it plainly, I was pissed! Jon opted to stay home with us, his family, as any decent husband and father would do. Besides, we didn't have the gas money to go anywhere. We were still very much destitute.

In May of 2001, as the rest of my college class graduated, I celebrated having a washer and dryer again. I wouldn't graduate until December because I had double majored in music education *and* performance. The extra major had inadvertently added an additional semester on to my life as a college student. Be that as it may, we had been without a washer or dryer for nine months. I found the appliances at a garage sale in Morrisonville and had managed to get the person that was selling them to also haul them home for me. We lived several miles from the nearest laundry and had only been able to go about once a month. Doing laundry once a month took around four hours to get it all washed, dried, and folded. School and work schedules, coupled with only having one car, didn't easily permit time for doing laundry.

The summer before I graduated was a particularly trying time for us. We were not able to buy groceries for an entire month. We were down to three stale tortillas and some mustard before we had any money freed up to buy groceries with. Little Jon finally ate the old tortillas out of desperation. Sara said, "If we would have had ketchup instead of mustard I would have eaten them." We were not yet knowledgeable of the many food pantries in Central Illinois that were available to us at this time.

Our problems refused to end there. The electricity in our kitchen was screwed up. We had to run huge extension cords across the kitchen to keep our fridge, dishwasher and microwave running. I heard someone call this "hotwiring" a house. Extension cords everywhere were *fun* because we'd always be tripping over them and unplugging the fridge. The added gamble of getting electrocuted while washing dishes was also exciting. I'm pretty sure that this was probably a major fire hazard as well. Jon would now have to become an electrician and figure this one out. Calling an electrician was clearly not an option under our financial circumstances.

Nearing the end of my college career I was so stressed and angry at my situation that I was seriously looking for a fight. I would have never started a fight, but I cherished the thought of finishing one if the opportunity ever presented itself. I imagined situations like being in a grocery store that was being robbed or perhaps seeing an old lady getting her purse stolen. I'd rush to the scene of the crime and pummel the lowlife scumbag senseless and become a heroine. I didn't really desire to be the heroine necessarily, that would be an added perk. I just wanted a legal excuse to beat the living crap out of someone. I needed to vent all my anger and the bad guy was going to get it all. The criminal would take the pounding for everyone who had ever done me wrong.

There was a rapist on campus. Now was my chance! I had many classes that didn't get out until after dark. I was a lone female walking across a big campus. If a rapist wanted to attack me so be it. Let's get it on. I was ready to rumble. I relished the thought of giving them a thrashing they would never forget. I planned what I would do. I would knock the rapist unconscious by repeatedly slamming their head into the concrete of the parking lot. If they were stupid enough to try and assault me near my car I would beat them unconscious and then run over their legs and pin them there until the police arrived to collect the bloody remains. I didn't carry a knife or a gun for protection. Shooting someone wasn't violent enough for me. What is one bullet wound compared to hundreds of bruises, lacerations and broken bones from a hand to hand combat situation? It was going to be all fists and fury.

I realized that they might have a gun or a knife. That didn't bother me. I'd disarm them and use their weapon against them. I'd beat them into submission then I'd order them to lay flat on the ground. If they made the smallest of moves I'd start shooting. First, maybe I'd shoot their leg. If they moved again, I'd shoot the other leg. If they persisted in moving, I'd shoot off their dick. That way they'd never be able to try and rape anyone again. If they only had a knife I'd have to cut off their privates and dispose of the appendage where it would never be found. I didn't want to kill them. I wanted them to live to remember me.

I found myself looking under every bush and behind every building for the rapist. I scanned the scene in front and to the sides of me. My ears targeted on the slightest of sounds. A leaf blowing down the sidewalk several feet away attracted my attention. I was not going to be surprised. I believe, by law, the rapist would have to throw the first punch or make the first act of aggression, but after that they were all mine. I realized that I may still be liable if I beat them beyond what was necessary to escape, but I'd worry about that later. Yes, I considered the fact that I might not win the fight with a rapist or other criminal. I even entertained the idea that they might kill me. However, I wasn't going down without giving them the fight of their life. Thank God, for all parties concerned, I never encountered the rapist. I didn't find out until 2005 that these feelings of grandeur, where a person feels invincible, can sometimes be labeled as bipolar disorder.

Four and a half years later on December 8, 2001, $25,000 in student loan debt, I walked across the stage and accepted my Bachelor of Music Degree. I never thought I would make it to this point financially. At the end of each semester, I had made a point to say goodbye to all my friends for fear I wouldn't be able to monetarily afford to continue. To them, it must have seemed that I was suicidal in telling them goodbye in such a sad manner, because I never told them the truth of my economic challenges. It was quite clear to me by now that Dr. Riley's original offer of a free ride through college was made null and void upon his death. I had spent the last seventeen years of my life trying to make up for my lost teen and young adult years. My inability to complete my college degree was the never appeased root of my *unfinished business*. Although I married, had children and functioned as a responsible adult, deep inside I still felt like I was eighteen, like I was missing something. Adults had intimidated me ever since my mother died. I didn't understand adults or their attitudes. Their important careers scared me. They were serious all the time. They didn't want to do anything fun. I lived to engage in recreation and try all sorts of new amusements. They were always too tired, too busy or too fearful of my preferred list of activities. I thought adults were boring. A magical transformation took place when they placed my degree in my hand. I was now free to be a thirty-seven year old woman. I had graduated into my rightful adulthood. I didn't have to be trapped with the mindset of an eighteen year old the rest of my life. However, as old as I was, it just wasn't the same without parents there to be proud of my accomplishments. I had sent out invitations to my sisters and to Jon's family. Only one of Jon's sisters showed up. I hadn't expected Karen to come. Karen's oldest daughter made a comment to the effect that she thought it was awful that Fran hadn't bothered to attend. I hadn't expected that any of them would come. The invitation was meant only as a polite gesture. By this time, I was disgusted with Jon's family and therefore, I wasn't that welcoming to Karen. I'm sure the feeling was mutual. Graduating from college felt rather empty.

Chapter Four: Graduation

Despite the odds, even with all that chaos in our lives, I had graduated with a degree in music education and music performance in the middle of December, 2001. This was my first problem. Schools do not hire teachers in December. Schools hire teachers in the summer. There were no teaching jobs in this area at present. If fact, they were laying off teachers locally. I suppose I could have done some substitute teaching, but I wasn't interested in babysitting someone else's class. More importantly, there is no guarantee that I would be called in to work! I might sub on Monday and then not be called again for two weeks. Substitute teachers are the bottom feeders, the scavengers of the teaching world. Subs have to lie in wait for other teachers to get sick or suffer some misfortune in order to get a few days of work here and there. Subbing was not an option. We had to have a steady income.

We would have moved, but we couldn't pay for the U-Haul truck. A credit card is required to rent a U-Haul and we no longer had a credit card. All of our cards had been turned over to collection agencies when we could no longer keep up with the monthly payments. There was also no way we could pay first and last month's rent on an apartment anywhere. Then, there are the fees for setting up utilities. Besides, I didn't relish the thought of living in rental properties again and I hate the city. I wanted my kids to be out here in the country where there are no gangs and you don't even have to lock your doors for the most part. I didn't want to sacrifice the freedom, peace and security that the location of my home afforded. I would have to wait until next summer, at the very least, to get a job teaching music.

The first job I took upon graduation was at a Christian daycare in Springfield. I had graduated on the 8th of December and had started my job on the 7th of December. There was no time to celebrate my graduation from college with a little rest and relaxation. There was no time to be picky. I had to take any job I could find. I had a family of four depending on me to feed them, put clothes on their backs and keep a roof over their head. That particular daycare only paid about $7.00 an hour. That little bit of pay was not going to support my family. Heck, seven lousy dollars an hour wouldn't support a single person living under a bridge in a cardboard box! To make matters worse, I was stuck in a room full of two year olds by myself all day.

Twos are the worst of all ages. They weren't potty trained and the bathroom was way down the hall, up a small flight of stairs and around the corner. Do you know how hard it is to single-handedly get a group of eight two year olds to walk in the same direction? I found a rope and tried to make them all hold on to it in a line so we could make it to the bathroom and back. Some of them refused to hold the rope at all. Some held the rope for awhile and then ran off in the opposite direction. Others would not stay in their place in line. Instead, they would go from the back of the line to the front of the line while still holding tightly to the rope. The rope would get all tangled up and kids would start falling down. This would lead to crying, whining, screaming, and attacking the child they thought had pushed them down. I don't know why the whole rope thing didn't work. It had worked at other daycare centers. Once inside the bathroom I had to help each child pull down their pants and lift them on to the adult-sized toilets. Some would hop off immediately and pee in their pants when we got back to the classroom. I guess I don't blame them. They were probably afraid they'd fall into such a huge toilet and be flushed away forever. A few of the children were not being potty trained so they would sit there bored to death during the whole process. I got wise and tried to make them look at books until we could go back to the classroom. This didn't work too well. It didn't entertain them long enough. The children who weren't using the toilets would spend their time in the bathroom opening up the cabinets underneath the sink, crawling underneath the stalls, swing the doors open and shut, flushing the toilets, or possibly sticking their hands in the toilet bowl. Without fail, a few of the children would try to escape from the bathroom and run around the church while I was in the process of wiping someone's butt. I really needed a teacher's assistant or at least a child-size toilet in my classroom.

Lunch time and breakfast time at the daycare was a mess. Each teacher was responsible for serving the food to their own classes. We were also responsible for cleaning up after them. Two year olds spill everything. It was not unusual for a child to need a complete change of clothes after breakfast or lunch. On top of all this, we were expected to sit at the table with the children and attempt to eat our own lunch. Sitting was an impossibility. The tables were knee high at best. The chairs were miniature. Neither was very comfortable. Sitting and eating was more like jumping up every two seconds to catch spills and separate fights. The fights were usually started because one child tried to take another child's food or perhaps as little as one child touching another child's chair. The other teachers at the daycare, who were largely on their own all day, seemed unwilling to help each other. Some seemed outright hostile if you so much as asked them to watch your room while you went to the bathroom.

This was a trying job, but not the worst job I would ever have. After all, they were only two years old and it is hard not to get attached to them on some level. I especially liked them when they were all asleep. Naptime, glorious naptime! I covered our only small window that we had in our classroom with dark construction paper and anything else I could find to obstruct the light. We were in the basement and had a wonderful view of the church parking lot so blocking the window was no great loss. It was so dark in that room you could have developed photographs. The kids couldn't see to move around so they had to stay in one place, on their cots. They still took longer than I had wanted for them to fall asleep. One boy in particular would continually get up, darkness or not. Why must there always be one or two that won't cooperate? I had to sit by them and pat them on their backs to make them stay on their cots until they fell asleep. What was really bad was when three or four children refused to lay down. I had only two arms to pat backs with. Sometimes it took over an hour until they were all asleep.

Daycares usually have some kind of music playing while the children sleep. I brought along a copy of my senior recital from Millikin and listened to it while I made lesson plans for the munchkins. I suppose it was my way of encouraging myself. I prayed that I would have a real job teaching music in a real school next school year.

My total darkness method worked rather well until one day when the daycare director walked in and saw how dark my room was. She told me I had to take some of the stuff off my window because if there were ever a fire I'd have to see the children to get them out. I figured if there was ever a fire we'd all die. I had already proven to myself that I was incapable of getting a classroom full of two year olds to walk in the same direction. I started to ponder this situation. Maybe if I just shoved each child out that small basement window they would escape a fire. No, they would probably get ran over seeing as how I'd be pushing them into a parking lot next to a busy street. I probably couldn't carry more than three kids in my arms at one time. That would mean that five kids would still be burned alive. I realized I couldn't save them all. Which ones would I save? How would I make such a decision? Would I leave behind the difficult, defiant children that tested me to no end and only take the obedient kids? I'd like to think that I wouldn't choose who lived and who died based on looks or personality. However, the obedient kids would probably be the ones to survive. I say that only because they would be more apt to follow my directions on how to get out of the building.

SPREAD THE PEANUT BUTTER THIN!

I had found some success in controlling these little guys though. They responded well to small candies like gummy bears. They would sit still and be quiet if they knew I had treats to give out. It seemed too similar to training a dog, but at this point I didn't care what it took. Candy was plentiful. We had a huge stash of it on hand from our recent Valentine's Day party; however, even though I had found a method to somewhat control the kiddies, I had to continue to look for a job that paid more.

I'm not really sure what kind of graduation presents other people get, but my graduation present from Millikin was a room full of screaming two year olds, poopy pants, diaper rash, low pay and no benefits.

I resigned from that particular daycare as soon as I was hired as a Head Start teacher on February 18, 2002.

Chapter Five: Death

I recall giving cans of food to food drives on different occasions throughout my life. I never dreamed that food pantries would someday be our primary source of groceries. What I had given in the past was about to come back to me many times over. I first learned about all the different food pantries in our area thanks to my job as a Head Start teacher. The Head Start program had a wonderful little booklet that listed all kinds of services in it. You could have all your needs met with this one little book titled, *The Family Yellow Pages.* It had everything from where all the food pantries were, to finding support groups of various kinds, to where to get free clothes and free furniture. What I learned about resources in my area from my job as a Head Start teacher eventually would save us from certain hunger.

    This job actually had some decent benefits, life, health, disability, dental and vision. I signed up for life and disability right away because they were freebies and it didn't come out of my paycheck. My family was still covered by Medicaid until August. The kids would continue to be covered by public aid for their medical needs until they turned nineteen or until I could bring us above the official poverty level, whichever came first. In August, I planned to enroll myself for the medical and dental insurance at work. I would have enrolled Big Jon, but then I wouldn't have much of a check left.

    I loved working with my co-teacher Miss Teena. She had worked there for a long time. She wanted to teach older children, but she felt that they had her stereotyped as an infant teacher only. We worked with babies from zero to age two. We got along well. We talked and laughed all day while taking care of the babies. We played every kind of music possible, all day long, for the babies. I liked a wide variety of genres so we had everything from Irish tunes to Spanish guitar compositions. I enjoyed swooping up a baby and dancing to the assortment of tunes. Life was starting to look good.

    Every afternoon the cook came by with the more than ample food for our little nursery school. The food was cooked in a different building, but it was brought to us hot and fresh. My compliments to the chef, definitely! It was all extremely good and the cook's use of seasonings was outstanding. Miss Teena said, "He seasoned the vegetables so good that it really made you feel like eating them." I personally loved his carrots. Miss Teena said the teachers used to take the surplus of leftovers home with them, but they weren't allowed to anymore. She was like me. She hated to see good food go to waste, especially when food could be so hard to come by.

    Miss Teena was laid off in April. Declining enrollment had sent her packing. I was shocked. I was the newbie. I should have been the first one laid off. I don't know why they kept me and not her. I was glad they did though. This job paid well and the people were pleasant for the most part.

    On certain days, my Bear would drop me off at the nursery, leave the car with me, and then catch a bus to go to his job at Burger King. He did this because he would be working until 7:00 p.m. and I needed to get to my second job by 5:00 p.m. One Wednesday morning, Bear was minding his own business waiting for a bus when a car pulled up in front of him and beckoned him to come over. He approached the car to see what they wanted. A man in the back seat asked him if he wanted some pussy. Then, a teenage girl in the front seat rolled down her window.

"What's up?"

My Bear answered, "Nothing was up," and they drove off.

My Bear was amazed at how abnormal our life was turning out. This was a poor and often corrupt side of Springfield. People were desperate and would do what they had to do to earn a buck.

Not too long after this incident, the manager at the Burger King went to pick up a new employee. He stopped when he saw a woman waving him down. The manager thought that the woman was the new employee he was supposed to pick up. It turned out to be another whore. The manager said it took awhile to get the hooker out of his car. Jon said that everyone was laughing behind the manager's back at work all day long. I deduced that Springfield sluts must prefer Burger King employees.

Once, as I was getting the babies ready to go home I saw a cop car pull up in the parking lot outside my window. One of the nicest dads was in my room picking up his baby. Before I knew it the policeman had burst into my classroom. He arrested the father, who remained calm, and cuffed him in front of all the children. I don't know why this happened. I do know that he could have waited until the father came outside the nursery school to arrest him instead of causing a commotion in front of all the babies and children.

The Head Start program was created for underprivileged preschoolers. As a result of the low income clientele there was a need for all types of assistance, including food. Once a week, someone from our little nursery school would go to the food bank and bring back a couple of car loads of food items for the convenience of the families we served. After the daycare families took what they wanted the teachers could have what was left. One time I got mostly bread. Another time we were given candy and plastic wraps. Yet another time we received snack crackers. Every little bit helped.

The teachers were paid above average wages, around $10.50 an hour, but as always I was the primary breadwinner. Jon was working at a Burger King for minimum wage part time. We were still in poverty according to United States standards, but we were doing okay. In fact, after just a few weeks of making this kind of money I was feeling at ease enough to announce that we could start planning to take a day trip to Six Flags in St. Louis. We planned our trip for the 25th of May. I found out on May the 14th that the 24th would be my last day at work. It seemed that the moment I decided that we were going to have a little discretionary income, I got laid off. I had worked at this particular Head Start school for three months, February 2002 through May 2002, when they told me goodbye.

It seemed like every summer we were in abject poverty. This was really getting old. At least the car had the decency to break down on us while I still had my job and could pay for the repairs. I spent about four hundred dollars on the car, one weeks worth of pay at my Head Start job, but at least I had it. Now, we had a car that ran, but soon we would have no gas money to go anywhere. What a kick in the pants! I told Sara I got laid off.

"I guess that means we aren't going to Six Flags," she sighed.

She knew the routine.

Groceries could be handled by the wealth of information on all the food pantries I had gathered. Electricity was a necessity. I would continue to pay that bill. Water was a necessity. I hoped it would rain. The telephone was a necessity if potential employers were going to be able to call me. I'd have to keep the phone on. The house payment was going to have to wait.

I told myself I was not going to get depressed this time, but despite my greatest attempts, I found myself not able to sleep more than three or four hours a night. Something about the possibility of losing your home will do that to a person. Just to think, I was so concerned about two weeks ago that Jon's job didn't have any benefits. I was worried about having to pay one quarter of my salary to cover Jon and the kids on the medical plan provided by the Head Start program. It looks like I didn't have to worry about that any more. At this current rate of poverty we are good for another year on the public aid medical card. It was time to hit the doctor up for some anti-depressants!

Little Jon was supposed to go to summer school this summer. I had to tell the school district that I couldn't take him or pick him up because it conflicted with my work hours. There was no bus service for summer school. We didn't have any neighbors who could take him. Little Jon desperately needed academic help, but I had to work! If I didn't go to work, Little Jon wouldn't eat or have a home to live in. I guess I could take him to summer school now that I was laid off, but enrollment was full. Little Jon had to do without the education he needed because I had to work. This wasn't fair. I thought work was meant to provide for your children's needs. I guess I was wrong about that. Little Jon really needed to be in a Sylvan Learning Center or the Dyslexic Institute or both. Sara and Little Jon needed academic help. Sara was dyslexic too. It was just one more thing we couldn't afford. Now, what was I going to do? My job as a Head Start teacher was gone.

I had graduated from college just five months previous to this lay off and had not worked at the Head Start program long enough to draw unemployment. We were doomed! We had no savings. We were living week to week. We had spent every last dime we had, quite literally, on getting my college degree. Actually, we had spent all that and more. I still owed over $25,000 dollars in student loans! Needless to say, we had to figure out how to survive until I could find another job. I had to assess what our most important needs were. At least I still had my gig at the music store.

At about the same time that I became a Head Start teacher I also started teaching private music lessons part-time at the House of Music in Springfield. Every night after work I would wait for Jon to pick me up and take me over to the music store where I taught private violin, viola and mandolin lessons. I had never played a mandolin in my life, but it was tuned just like a violin so I figured what the heck. If the boss man wanted me to teach mandolin, then I guess I would teach mandolin. I had a family to support and I was not about to quibble over formalities. Besides, this was music, my preferred way to make money. The owner of the store was a shrewd, hardworking and sometimes acidic older man. I never had any problems with him, but I had seen him chew out some of his other employees. I'd also seen him get into it with his customers too!

His store, which was actually an old house, was crammed full of merchandise. He also owned two or three more adjacent houses that held pianos and even more supplies. He literally had anything that you might ever need as a musician. He even had strange Australian indigenous instruments hanging on the wall for sale. I'm not sure that there is a great need for Aboriginal instruments in central Illinois, but if the occasion ever came up for one it was there. Some of his sheet music dated back to the 1930's! Apparently, he never threw away anything. It was not the kind of store where you just browsed. Someone had to help you find what you needed. Otherwise, you might get lost, covered in a landslide of dusty instruments or marching band arrangements from the 1970s. There was hardly room to walk.

I taught lessons upstairs in a practice room that was just as crowded as the rest of the store. I was paid $8.00 for every one hour lesson I taught. My boss charged my students $12.00 an hour and he kept $4.00 as his cut. This was agreeable.

On certain nights, I would have to wait for a ride home from the music store. We only had one car and Jon usually had it. When the music store closed I would walk across the street to a small gas station and wait. The Clark gas station was just as small and cramped as the music store was. This was the bad side of town, but that didn't bother me. The Head Start program I worked at was on the bad side of town too. I spoke to the man that was working at the gas station a bit. He was painting, trying to brighten up the nicotine stained walls, when I walked in. He didn't mind if I waited for my ride there. A woman walked in and made some comment about not getting the right change back for a pack of cigarettes she had bought there. The gas station attendant told her to get out and explained to me that this woman came in all the time with this same story. She was only trying to get money for her drugs.

About one month later, the gas station attendant was kidnapped, beaten, and shot while at work. It was Tuesday, March the 26th. He died the next morning. His body was hauled out into the country, near Rochester, about seven miles from where I lived and dumped. Some local teenagers found his remains in a ditch. The gas station where I used to wait was now outlined in yellow crime scene tape. I guess I was lucky that I had not been there the night he was shot. They might have found my body thrown along side the road too. Then again, if I had been there the outcome might have been totally different. I could have waged war against the gunman and been the heroine. God knows I still had enough anger issues that the fight would have been a good one. The gunman may possibly have been dead instead of the gas station attendant.

One month after I was laid off, I was hired back. It was now June 2002 and this time I would be at a different location teaching three and four year olds in the Head Start program. I enjoyed this new location even more than the nursery school. The facility was very attractive and there was an abundance of toys and supplies. There was no pay increase or added benefits, but that didn't matter. I didn't expect any. The food was still good and the coworkers were great. The assistant teacher in my room was Miss Selena. We got along well, too. We spent lots of time taking walks around the neighborhood with the children.

Some of the children here had problems. I'm not sure if they were acting out on what they saw at home or what. I had children throw chairs, cuss, kick and hit me, or at least try to. Sometimes they landed a kick that I didn't catch. It was no big deal for me. How hard can a little kid kick anyway? There was a lot of anger in some of these preschoolers.

My house was a mess. I tried to force myself to clean house some before I went to work each day. Otherwise, I'd get home to late, around 9 pm, to do anything around the house. It would all pile up for one, big, overwhelming mess on the weekends. The last thing I wanted to do was clean the stupid house all day long on the weekends when I've been working two jobs all week long. Usually, I cleaned for about four hours on Sunday and what didn't get done just didn't get done. Sometimes I just said, "Forget it."

I wanted the weekend off so, I didn't clean at all for two weekends in a row. Then, I'd have all kinds of health-violating filth awaiting me when I did get enough energy to clean. It really got nasty, but I could only do so much. Big Jon, as always, failed to recognize how much a messy house stressed me. Subsequently, he didn't succeed in cleaning like he should have. Cleaning the house was and is the biggest argument we have. Jon didn't really see the need for cleaning. I couldn't relax and unwind in a dirty house. God knows I needed a place to slow down somewhere. The kids did help, but during the school year they didn't get home from school until 5:00 p.m., thanks to their hour long bus ride, and then they had homework. They couldn't do much cleaning on weekdays, there wasn't any time. The kids were doing good to make themselves something for dinner. Their favorite quick fix was ramen noodles or frozen french fries. Sometimes, they'd open up a can of chicken noodle soup or make some macaroni and cheese.

We were now behind two months in our house payments. The bank was not interested in partial payments. They wanted all or nothing. I had no choice. I didn't have all of it. So, I sent nothing.

It was now July. I had been back to work for one month. We were still not back on our feet from the month I had no income. The house payment was now three months behind. The bank wouldn't work with me. It was still all or nothing. The bank was ready to throw us out of our home.

As July turned into August, I had no idea if I should enroll my kids in the school where they went last year or not. I had no idea where we might be living in a few weeks! This was not good! Sara, age fifteen, was more than a bit upset. Little Jon, always the mellow child, was twelve and seemed ignorant of the ramifications of our impending doom. Bear, seemingly always believing that someone would rescue him from such a crisis, didn't seem to sense the magnitude of our situation either. I was over burdened and stressed. I had to carry all the weight and I resented it! I didn't know what to do and Bear didn't have any viable ideas. Bear was working about 35 hours a week at Burger King, but he made only $600.00 a month. We had no credit cards or I would have went to the nearest bank and obtained a cash advance to cover the over due house payments. We had no savings. Jon had depleted his IRA to cover living expenses while I was in college. We couldn't borrow against an IRA that no longer existed.

To make matters worse, since Jon's mom still didn't have our phone number she was getting paranoid. She started sending her personal mail for Jon to the Burger King! Obviously, Fran did not realize that Jon's job at Burger King did not come with his own office, a personal assistant and private mail delivery. Was she seriously trying to get Jon fired or was she just that out of it? Fran had become convinced that I wasn't giving Jon his mail when she sent it to our house. *His* mail? Any mail that comes into this house is for *everyone* to see. Believe me, if Fran wrote to Jon he'd hear about it, over and over and over again. Her trivializing letters pissed me off to no end! She always had some overly simplified, flippant, and often erroneous, solution to all our problems.

Occasionally, Fran would enclose a small check with her letter or card. She didn't want Jon to let me have the money she sent for him. Why? Who knows? Did it matter who eventually held the money in their hands. It was going to be spent on toilet paper, trash bags, gasoline, or some other necessity. Was it really that important to Jon's mom as to which one of us went to the store and bought the monthly feminine supplies with her money? Fran must have been thinking that her small gifts were just that, a gift. She must have intended for Jon to go and buy himself something that he would like with the money. She still didn't get it. We were too destitute to consider things we might want. We had to focus on getting what we needed.

Be that as it may, let's consider the situation at hand. Everyone at Burger King is making low wages. Most of the workers are probably eligible for public assistance unless they have a spouse that makes good money. They just barely exist. There are also many unscrupulous people that work at low paying jobs. Even a thirty dollar check is a fortune to minimum wage workers. Jon is extremely lucky that he received his mail at all, once the people at Burger King had it in their paws. Only God knows how many of his little gifts might have been stolen.

I went to work on August the 12th as usual. At approximately 8:45 in the morning, I was walking down the hall when I heard Ms. Miranda, another teacher, say that someone was outside "dying". I said, "dying?" and proceeded to the front door to see what was going on. I thought she was exaggerating. I was thinking that maybe I'd find someone having a severe asthma attack or something similar. Immediately outside the front door was a gray car and a lady was lying on the ground beside it. Several people were just standing around either not knowing what to do or too much in shock to do anything. I checked the woman's pulse at the wrist and at her neck. I felt no pulse. I observed that when I touched her neck that she made two short and shallow gasps. I then noted that she made no further efforts to breathe. Her eyes were glazed and not focused. Miss Brianna, another coworker, and I began CPR. I breathed for the lady and Miss Brianna did the heart compressions. After each breath I heard a gurgling sound come from the woman's throat. I hoped to God that she wouldn't throw up on me. I remember turning around briefly, looking at the crowd and asking, where the ambulance was. The paramedics were there just as soon as I spoke. One of the paramedics took my name and address. I watched for a few minutes longer and then went to my classroom. I found the bottle of hydrogen peroxide and rinsed my mouth several times. As much as I had been eager to help, I didn't want to catch anything either. You would have thought that they would suggest I go home after having been through that ordeal. They didn't suggest it and I went back to my classroom and did my job as usual.

    I don't know why I didn't have a nervous break down or at least one of my anxiety attacks that I have had periodically since I was eighteen years old. I suppose when you are in the middle of the battle you don't think about taking the time to panic. You just do and keep on doing.

    I found out later that the woman we had tried to help had died. Apparently, she had a known heart condition. She had a massive heart attack and there wasn't anything anyone could do. I didn't catch the woman's name, but several days later one of my coworkers told me that a relative had told her to thank me for what I had done. What had I done? My first time to ever do CPR and the patient had died! I was hoping that she would have lived. I hoped that it wasn't me who had done something wrong. I was recently trained in adult, infant and child CPR as well as first aid, but still. I don't think I did the breathing wrong. I saw her chest rising up and down. I guess we tried.

    It was mid August 2002. My house was still going to be foreclosed on. Jon finally broke down, in desperation, and asked his mother for monetary help in saving our home. Surely she would help. She was a person of significant means. Rumor has it that Fran had been left millions by her late husband, Jon's dad. Exactly how many millions of dollars was unclear. All of his relatives, on the whole, were doing extremely well for themselves. They would hear of my plight and have compassion. I was a female, head of household, trying my best to provide for a family and hang on to our home. They would honor and applaud my fortitude. They would respect me for that fact that I hadn't divorced Jon's butt long ago. In essence, I was like a single mom with no husband to provide any kind of substantial income. Yes, most other women would have cut and run. When the man no longer makes the money the woman usually doesn't stay around long. Jon hadn't had a professional job or even a halfway livable income in about six years now. My mother-in-law would rise to my aid and exalt my determination to stay with her son. All my in-laws would laud me and sing my praises because I had worked so hard to get through college with two young children at home. They were all good *Christians*. They would be understanding and be consoling. I had stepped in to be the breadwinner when Jon either wouldn't or couldn't anymore. My innocent children had suffered so much that the in-laws surely would not hear of them having to be uprooted and thrown on the streets two weeks before school started. They would rush to our side to support us in our time of need. They would band together with me as any loving and caring family would. When everyone else walks out, your family walks in. Your family is always in your corner. Family is the one thing you can count on. Yeah, right…Our cry to save our home was met with a "No."

Instead, we were offered accommodations in Jon's childhood home in Big Spring, Texas. One of Jon's recently divorced, male cousins, whom I honestly did not know, already lived in this house. I was not about to clean up after anyone else! If his own wife didn't want him, I sure didn't want him either. I didn't need more drama. If we didn't want to move in with his cousin, we had the option of moving into one of Fran's rental houses, also in Big Spring. We didn't know anyone in Big

Spring! Jon hadn't lived there in over thirty years! It was close to a thousand miles away! The poverty rate in west Texas was insane! There were absolutely no jobs in Big Spring! This small town had been on the decline for years! We'd move to Big Spring and seriously have to live on welfare the rest of our lives!

Big Spring was a godforsaken desert wasteland filled with dust storms, Africanized killer bees, scorpions, rattlesnakes, cacti and fire ants! Little Jon was allergic to fire ants! He had been attacked by those tiny, six-legged beasts when he was a toddler. I had been in our backyard, in Grand Prairie, Texas, mowing the grass. Every time the mower ran over even the smallest of fire ant mounds, those demonic creatures would swarm up from the ground and latch on to my shoes and legs. Their mounds can range in size from an eighth of an inch high to ten inches high and just as wide, or more! Their bite was a sharp pain followed by severe itching. The pesticide they sold in the hardware stores didn't harm them. I'd sprinkle the yellow, insecticide granules on top of their mound and they'd just move the mound to a different location within twenty-four hours. I heard that to really kill these insects you had to hire an exterminator and pay major money. Even though Big Jon had been making a livable income as a computer programmer, this was something we couldn't manage to pay for. Little Jon had been standing on our small, concrete back porch. I didn't realize that the fire ants had a big mound right next to the concrete. By the time I realized what was going on, his legs were covered with ants! I stripped his clothes off of him outside, brushed the ants off with my hands and rushed him to the nearest clinic. His legs were bright red and swollen! At the clinic, a foreign, female doctor started to lecture me about how different religions are against medical intervention. What?! The lady was a nut! If I was anti-medication did she think I would be standing here? She then proceeded to tell me that she had seen worse cases where the child's entire body had swollen up and they died. Was she going to help me or did I need to take Little Jon somewhere else? I didn't have time to play games like this! This chick must have missed the part about reassuring the patient when she was studying to be a doctor. She finally gave him a shot of something to stop the allergic reaction. Little Jon spent the next few days with huge, hard welts all over his legs. I didn't relish the thought of moving to Big Spring where he might be assaulted by these monsters again.

When we used to visit Fran in Big Spring, before she had moved into her retirement home, we'd always find a scorpion crawling around on the floor in one of the back bedrooms. I had never been stung by one and I didn't intend to start now. Hadn't I heard somewhere that those mutant roaches with stingers can kill people? I could only imagine what would happen if Sara or Little Jon got stung by a scorpion! It wasn't a pleasant thought.

Jon's dad had been a medical doctor, with a thriving practice, specializing in arthritis. As the story goes, his dad had always loved the mountains. His mom had always wanted a home by the beach. They had the means to have lived anywhere they wanted. The world was theirs! So, they bought a house in Big Spring?! What kind of compromise was this? Neither one got what they wanted. Instead, they lived in an area that literally looked like it had been nuked! Why anyone would want to live in a parched region where the grass didn't grow and trees were stunted to the size of bushes was beyond me. Big Spring was a landscape of hell. I already had enough hell in my life without physically living there.

Sara hurried to her room and produced all the money she had been saving from birthdays and Christmases ever since she was a baby. Good girl! Naively, Sara had thought she had been saving this money to go to college some day. I didn't have the heart to tell her that at our current financial status she would probably never be able to go to college. Little Jon retrieved his stash of savings from his bedroom as well. We counted all the money up. If I put all their money with my paycheck we could save the house. With a promise to pay them back, I accepted their money. We did what we had to do. School started in two weeks!

We literally used all the money we had to save the house. Every last cent was gone. This money got us caught up in back payments. Now, I couldn't afford the current month's house payment. The bank was okay with us being one month behind on payments, but I didn't have any margin of error left. A mortgage payment had to be made every month. If the car broke down or if anything else happened it was just too bad. I couldn't afford to take care of it because I had to make the house payment. With my low paying jobs I wasn't able to get current on the house payments. We would continually stay a month behind in our payments for the next two years!

Chapter Six:
The Rain Dance

Due to all the lay offs at the Head Start program, I was already searching for other employment. It wasn't just the lay offs that bothered me. I had spent four and a half years in college to become a music teacher, not a preschool teacher. I taught in daycares *before* I went to college! As much as I loved working at the Head Start program, surely, I was worthy of something more than working in a daycare the rest of my life. There were hardly any openings for music teachers. However, I did manage to get an interview with a school in Decatur. They were ready to hire me. This might have been good news for anyone else. I mean you have to start your chosen career somewhere. For me, this was not all good news. The position paid only $9.33 an hour. I would have to take a pay cut. The Head Start program paid a dollar an hour more than the Decatur school. Furthermore, Jon would have to quit working except for weekends if I accepted this job. We had one car and the round trip from Decatur, where I would be working, to Springfield, where Jon worked, twice a day wasn't worth it in driving time or gas money. I would also have to quit my part time job at the music store in Springfield for the same reason. A round trip from Decatur to drop me off, to Springfield for his work at the Burger King, and then back to Decatur to pick me up would have been a horrific commute. This would have been a total of about 160 miles or three hours and fifteen minutes of drive time every day! Gasoline prices were ridiculously high the summer of 2002, approaching two dollars a gallon, and this was not feasible. Little did we know that two bucks a gallon for gas would be cheap in just a few short years! My commute to Decatur and back home would be about forty-five minutes each way. Buying a second car, even the cheapest of used cars, was not within our means.

I accepted the job as music teacher and begged Jon to look for a job in Decatur. I thought "Director of Instrumental Music", my new title, would look better on a resume than "preschool teacher" when I tried to find a better paying teaching job the subsequent school year. I was forever looking for the next opportunity, determined to bring my family up from the abyss of poverty that had sucked us in. There was a hole in my theory of upward mobility. Most of the public school systems locally were either cutting back on non-essential classes such as music and art or they had already cut them.

The job at the Decatur school looked innocent enough initially. I was to teach third through eighth grade instrumental music. I had an orchestra, three levels of band, and a jazz band. Perfect! I loved the variety. I had only one week before school started to solidify my goals for the year. I began decorating and familiarizing myself with my office. I had an office! "Only important people have their own offices," I said to myself. Therefore, I must be important! I was told that the music program was valued at this school. Great! I was happy to be there.

It was my first teacher's meeting of the year. School was due to start in a few days. All the teachers and the principal were assembled around three tables, which were placed in a horseshoe outline. There were refreshments. I helped myself to a bagel and sat down. No sooner did I sit down than the vocal music teacher, who was sitting on my right, jumped back and squashed a bug.

"What was it?" another teacher asked.

"It looks like a flea," she replied.

I knew the flea had come from me. Yes, I'll admit it. I had fleas! Maybe I wasn't covered in them, but an occasional flea still resided on me. I was extremely embarrassed. However, I gave my best acting performance ever. I wrinkled my eyebrows in disgust as if to ask, "Where did a flea come from?" The commotion I had inadvertently caused dissipated as quickly as it had erupted. The other teachers never suspected that I had been the guilty party.

How did I get fleas? From my St. Bernard, Buhungo, of course. Buhungo was born to be an inside dog. If we didn't let him in the house he'd paw at our huge picture window. He had already broken the window in our kitchen by "knocking" on it. We hadn't had the cash to replace it yet. We had a choice. Let him and his fleas inside or have another broken window.

The cheap flea killers they sell in the grocery stores don't work very well and I didn't have the money to buy the expensive stuff, that actually works, from the veterinarian's office. Every room in my house was thoroughly infested with fleas. They were so bad that they had even taken over my bed. I got into the habit of vacuuming my bed and spraying myself with Off before I went to sleep at night. You could actually hear the fleas jumping around on the floor. It sounded like a miniature hailstorm. When we sat in the living room to watch television the fleas would attach themselves to our socks. Everyone in the house had several itchy red spots on their ankles. I knew dogs could get tapeworms from fleas. I wondered if humans could get worms from fleas too. Wasn't the black plague caused by fleas that had bitten infected rodents? We had plenty of rodents outside, and occasionally inside, our house. If we didn't acquire the hantivirus from the mouse droppings in my kitchen cabinet, we'd surely get the plague from the fleas.

I prayed that the Department of Child and Family Services never had reason to come to my house. One look at all these fleas and my children would be in foster homes. I was sure that this must constitute child abuse or neglect.

The fleas preferred breeding ground was a pile of dirty laundry that was in the living room. Our well water supply was always limited so the clothes had not been washed for a long period of time. Buhungo had decided that this particular pile of laundry was his doggie bed. That was fine with me. For the most part, these were clothes that we didn't wear, but hadn't had the time to sort through. The fleas had laid their eggs all over them. Maybe I should say they cemented their eggs to the garments. The oval-shaped, white eggs did not come off in the wash. Sometimes you could scrape them off, but it was almost impossible. We eventually discovered that the purple-colored, spray can of Raid kills these little monstrous devils. This celebrated bit of knowledge did not come to us until we had lived through several months of being eaten alive by the parasites.

Meanwhile, at work, there was a storm brewing. I don't really know how or why it started. I do know that it had started long before I ever arrived at this school and I'm positive that it continued after I was gone. I liked the actual job, but some of the people I had to contend with were not so nice. Most of the other teachers were nice enough. Some of the parents were another story. There seemed to be a group of mothers that were always hanging around the school. In a day and age where much emphasis is put on parental involvement, or lack thereof, this should have been a good thing. Without going in to too much detail, I will just say that these parents had decided that since they were paying for their children to attend this school, they would also tell the teachers how to teach and what grade their child should receive. If a teacher disagreed with a parent, the teacher was always on the losing end. The parents were paying customers and it was our job to give the customer whatever they wanted. The teacher's were nothing more than pawns, slaves of a sort. The parent's paid your salary, so in essence, the parents owned the teachers. A couple of the teachers that had been there a long time said it hadn't always been like this. The teachers used to be respected, once upon a time. A third teacher, who was nearing retirement, was so upset by the actions of some of these parents that she actually broke down and cried over the way they treated her. I thought that this drama would surely pass over me. After all, music is the fun class. No one should have issues with the music teacher. I was wrong.

This job was turning out to be a nightmare. First, one of the parents accused me of preferring the orchestra students over the band students. Then, I was accused of slamming the phone in someone's ear. I was never told which parent I had allegedly hung up on so I had no idea who to apologize to. Petty little things like this occurred daily. I was constantly being hauled into the office and having my butt chewed. I started dreading going to work.

During this time we had a white, Chevy Lumina, 4-door, sedan, gas-guzzler with a tire that had a slow leak. I couldn't afford to replace the tire so I had to put air in it every other day. This went on for about nine months until I finally came up with the money to buy a tire. There is nothing like trying to fill up a tire all the time in a sub-zero Illinois winter. Air hoses are just about the slowest devices ever made! I made a point to be acquainted with every gas station that had free air between my home and Decatur. I can't believe that some gas stations wanted to charge for air! We needed a miracle!

On the other hand, we had a much more pressing issue than a leaky tire. An ongoing hardship we faced was lack of water. We live in the country and have a well. If it doesn't rain you simply don't have water. This usually isn't a problem for most people. Normal people just load up their water tank on the back of their truck and go in to the nearest town to fill it up. We didn't have a truck or a tank. Still, we could have called the water hauler. The water hauler, a redneck Bubba who owned an old fire engine, would bring water to your home and dump it in your well for about $30.00 a load. This much will last about two weeks or more. The only problem with this is we didn't have the $30.00. We had previously bought two loads of water and wrote a check for $60.00. That check had bounced. Water hauler man had sent the check back through the bank only to have it bounce again. Now, to get any water we would have to pay the $60.00 we owed from before plus the $30.00 for the new load. I didn't have $90.00!

Now, I don't know how this biological oddity happened, but for some reason I rarely have underarm odor. My father didn't have any odor and *never* wore deodorant. I may need to use deodorant once a month or less. Likewise, my sister Barbara had been blessed with stench-free armpits. The scientific community should study my pits so they can develop a vaccine to prevent stinking or at least a better deodorant. Of course, they should pay me handsomely, feed me gourmet dinners and put me up in a five star hotel for the duration of the study. My underarm's are worth it! In all seriousness, this peculiarity was a godsend during our periods of water shortages!

On the other hand, Jon really needs to bathe twice a day, preferably in Lysol, and use deodorant each time! Obviously, not having water was a much bigger problem for Jon. Granted, I felt grungy and uncivilized without a shower. Added to this, we didn't have a working air-conditioner at home and the school wasn't air-conditioned either! It wasn't right to stew in your own sweat, day after day, and not be able to bathe! It just wasn't fair that a *professional* teacher should not have showered before going to work. I guess no one ever said life was fair yet, did they? I was exasperated! My job didn't even pay enough for me to have water or an air-conditioner in my house!

When I was in college, one of the professors addressed the hygiene issue among poor students. She warned us not to be surprised when underprivileged kids come to school dirty because their water had been turned off. She never said anything about the teachers having to go to work grubby! I was starting to realize that work didn't pay a living wage any more. Once again, I was working full-time and was still on state assistance, public aid, call it welfare if you must. Surely, my life was just a nightmare that I would wake up from.

Several months later, Jon had a solution to our shower problem. It had been several days since he had bathed. It was raining. We lived in the middle of nowhere. No one would see him if he went outside with a bar of soap. We laughed at the absurdity of the idea. I went to bed. It was a nice December night. It was about forty degrees outside, which is mild for Illinois in December. I was soon asleep. Around four in the morning I woke up. Jon was standing in the bedroom wrapped in a towel. He looked a tad bit on the cold side. Then it hit me. "You didn't! He did! Oh my God! Did anyone see you? I can't believe you did that! Oh my God!"

Jon had stripped down to his birthday suit and bravely faced the cold, light, misting rain in order to take a shower. Jon found that standing directly under our broken downspout by the carport rewarded him with more water, but it was also much colder than the small, soft, rain droplets that fell from the sky. He opted to stand out in the driveway where we park our car instead. There was thunder and lightning in the far distant sky. Jon found the infrequent, gentle breeze was bearable, but unpleasant. Most of the cats were asleep under the carport where it was dry. They surely thought their owner had lost his mind.

About two years after Jon's strip tease boogie, I learned about financial hardship scholarships at the YMCA. I'm not sure how I found out about this, but the important thing was that the YMCA had locker rooms. In those locker rooms were showers! For ten dollars a month, the cost of a reduced rate Y.M.C.A. membership, my family could shower to their heart's content.

Lack of water was an enormous problem! This was quite obvious after Jon's naked little rain dance. I never fully understood the critical importance of water before. Now, whenever I watch those television specials pleading for money to benefit some third world country, I can really relate. I've been there without ever leaving Illinois! This is especially true if they mention building wells or lack of clean water to drink, bathe and cook with. It isn't that I didn't care before. That isn't it at all. In fact, I am a giver by nature. I'm not saying that to brag. I just love to give. It's a rush! The feeling I get when I give gifts to people in need is like a child opening presents on Christmas morning. I have heard many preachers say, "You can't outgive God." I believe God keeps track of what you provide willingly and cheerfully to others. If you meet a time of need in your life God will reimburse you. I believe God looks at your motives when you help out those less fortunate than yourself. If you are giving to receive some sort of recognition, God doesn't respect that. If you give with generosity and unselfishness, I think God credits your account with the same amount of money or goods that you donated. Not only this, but He will actually give you an incredible rate of return on it. I know that we received much more assistance during our hardship than we ever gave.

I have always known that it is better to give than to receive. Before all this tragedy hit my family I had a very naïve understanding of this. My former understanding was that it is better to give because giving is much more fun than receiving. I was thinking about Christmas presents and birthday presents. It is more satisfying to give a Christmas present than to receive one that is the wrong color, incorrect size, out of fashion or otherwise. Maybe you just didn't like the present you received. It wasn't your style or you already had one just like it. All of these reasons would make giving a much better option than receiving presents you really didn't want. I always felt awkward trying to act as if I liked a gift someone gave me when in actuality I didn't like it at all. If I gave the unwanted present to Goodwill then I feared that the giver would come to my house and want to see the present. Yes, it was much preferable to give than to endure these unwelcomed presents. After a few years of abject, third world style, poverty it became quite clear to me that giving was *so* very much better than receiving. Only this time, I had a new, more mature understanding of the whole concept; if you are the giver, then you are usually not in dire need.

Our income was so pitiful that we couldn't even buy groceries. We had just learned about the many food pantries that were available in our area from my job at the Head Start program and we were now frequent patrons. Before we knew about the food pantries, we were frankly staring starvation in the face. Actually, in the United States of America they don't call it starvation, they call it being *food insecure*. I don't know what we would have done without the help. We were very desperate. Poverty was a pest. It's a disease that attacks the whole body, mind and spirit of its unwilling hosts.

Speaking of pests, we thought we had finally rid ourselves of our moth infestation that had plagued us for several years. We were swarmed by tiny moths that apparently entered our house by way of a bag of dog food we had purchased some years ago. The moths invaded our foodstuffs on a regular basis. Just when we thought they were gone we would open up a box of cereal, their favorite food, and there they were. They would chew a hole into a box or sack and lay their eggs. The eggs would hatch into small white worms with black heads. The worms would eat the surrounding food until they matured. I couldn't afford to play games with these winged devils! Food was very hard to come by in our house. I opened up a bag of rice. The moths had decided they wanted my rice. I saw them as extra protein. I picked them out one by one. I cooked it. We ate it. We lived. I had to do whatever it took. Nothing could be wasted!

Despite all the negativity at work, we accomplished a lot in the instrumental music department that year. On September 11th, the band honored the victims of the World Trade Center, the Pentagon, and the flight that went down in Pennsylvania by playing a patriotic piece by the school flagpole. The band played this piece after only three rehearsals together. I'm quite sure that very few of the students had even touched their instruments all summer. I expected a lot from the band and they delivered for me. Solo and Ensemble contests were more than terrific. We received a bag full of superior medals at each contest! Each and every one of my students that went to contests received at least one superior first place medal. My beginning string class had a Christmas concert at a local upscale department store after just three months of lessons. They were adorably cute and well applauded. Our February concert was a great success. Two of my students were quite good on their flute solos they played after only three weeks of instruction! Most students would, in no way, be prepared to play a concert after just three weeks of instruction yet I presented the entire beginning band on at least one song. I also enjoyed playing trombone with my jazz band on one of the charts at our concert. I have always loved music. Teaching music was not a job to me. It was pleasure. I was in my element.

The entire time I had worked at that little Decatur school we had been surviving by going to the many food pantries for groceries. Buying groceries was out of the question for us. We were dependant on handouts. We had been reduced to begging, quite literally. During Christmas, the school had a food drive. Every morning I opened the doors to see sacks of food lining both sides of the hallway. Every morning it was all I could do not to take some of those sacks and load them up into the trunk of my car. I was the first one to arrive at the school. Who would see me? Who would notice just one sack missing? Every day the students kept bringing more and more food. It was torture! No one would notice. The temptation was real. Worse than the temptation was the idea that a professional would be having these thoughts. I consoled myself with the truth that all these groceries would be mine eventually. I would just have to make the trip to the food pantry to get them. It would be so much easier just to take them now! It would save the school the trouble of finding parents that had the time and the vehicles to transport the food to the food pantry. It was a hard sell to tell my food insecure self not to do it. Now here was a legitimate allegation none of the parents had picked up on. I was guilty of wanting to steal their food donations! I watched regretfully as the students loaded all that magnificent food on the trucks.

Food wasn't our only problem. We had no heater in our house! Our central heating and air-conditioning unit had given up the ghost several years ago. We hadn't had the money to repair or replace it. The charge for a service call was beyond our grasp. We relied on a wood-burning stove, which sat in our living room, as our only source of heat. In the winter, we had to haul heavy logs inside the house to keep warm. The logs, along with snow, ice and mud, would leave a mess all over the floor.

The constant smoke and dust weren't good for Little Jon's or Sara's asthma. I had asthma as well. This, along with Big Jon's reluctance to *ever* clean the house, was an asthmatics nightmare. This peeved me more than anything! I could be poor. I could deal with him not working outside the home. I could *not* handle him doing absolutely nothing inside the home all day. If I had to be the breadwinner, then he had to be the househusband. The wife is supposed to be the *helpmate* according to the Bible. The helper, in any situation, does less work than the owner of the business. The helper is there to tie up the lose ends. I was doing everything it seemed. *I* needed a helpmate! Our roles had done a complete reversal and he wasn't living up to his end of things. I felt like a single mom.

With the wood stove burning during the winter months, the house visibly collected enough dust to need dusting twice a day! You could write your name in the dust on the furniture in the morning, wipe it clean, and by evening you could write your name in the new dust that had collected. I didn't have time to dust the house. I was at work. When I finally made it home at night I was exhausted. It didn't help that I was constantly being criticized at work. I'd come home in a bad mood every day. I'd take the first half hour or so to let off steam. I'd report to Jon what the principal, or some parent, had accused me of today. It was all I could do to force myself to fix dinner and go to bed.

The stove heated our home fairly well, but the heat never did quite make it down the hall to the back bedrooms. Sara and Little Jon eventually got space heaters for their bedrooms. If no one was home all day, the fire would die out and we'd come home to an unbearably cold house. The temperature inside would drop to the forties! The same was true in the evenings while we slept. Jon and I slept with at least two sleeping bags and several blankets on our bed. We slept fully clothed and sometimes wore our coats to bed too. The alarm clock rang at five in the morning. It was torture for me to leave the warm bed and change clothes in the frigid air. I wasn't a morning person anyway and this wasn't helping.

I had to hit the road by six o'clock in order to be at school and teach my first class by seven. It was pitch black outside; the stars were still out as I turned out of the driveway. It was actually rather beautiful outside. Everything was still and quiet. There were usually very few other cars out at this time. The best part about the drive into Decatur wasn't the silence and peacefulness. It was the car's heater. The sun would just start to break as I approached the school's parking lot. There I was. It was the start of a new day. New opportunities to be griped out awaited me inside. God help me. Let me get through this day without anyone submitting another grievance against me. At least the school had heat.

I'd let myself inside the school. There were still a few minutes before seven o'clock. I'd head down to the tiny bathroom to quickly wash up in the sink. We normally didn't have water at home so this was the best I could do. I'd lock the door and give myself a sponge bath with the paper towels and soap. I needed to wash my hair, but we can't have *everything* we want now can we? "We can't have anything we *need*, much less want," I thought out loud.

We *needed* firewood at home and couldn't afford to buy any. The last load of wood we bought was too green and hadn't given off much heat. The thermostat dial on our wood burning stove had three burn indicators; creosote, burn zone and over fire. Creosote meant it was freezing cold inside the house. Burn zone meant that there was some lukewarm air coming out of the stove, but you better not take your coat off just yet. What I wouldn't have done for a little "over fire." Now, we had to resort to burning yard waste and household trash to keep warm. We'd fill grocery bags with dried leaves and small sticks for kindling. Junk mail and bills we couldn't pay were good fire starters too. We'd scavenge our yard for larger branches to keep the fire burning once we got it started. We'd jump on the larger branches to break them so they would fit in the stove. It was an uphill battle. We'd spend an hour outside to glean enough wood and debris for a half hour of warmth. Jon wore several layers of shirts. I found it easier to just wear my coat inside the house. I figured there had to be a bright side. Oh, I know! If we died from carbon monoxide poisoning due to the improperly sealed wood burning stove, our bodies would stay perfectly frozen until Spring. This would give someone enough time to find us before we started to attract flies.

We had plenty of wood on our four and a half acre spread, but there was no chain saw to cut it with. If only I could buy a chain saw for Jon for Christmas. By chance, I heard about the WYMG Christmas Wish. WYMG was a radio station from Springfield. You could nominate yourself or someone else if you needed extra help for Christmas. I sent them an email and told them about our situation. Much to my surprise, they called me at work and told me I had been selected to receive my Christmas Wish. They were going to send me a check for $400.00 to buy the chain saw. God was supplying our needs. He knew we were cold.

The check arrived in the mail within a day or two.

Our St. Bernard, Buhungo, had been acting sick. One of his eyes seemed to be clouded! We hadn't expected this. He wasn't even two years old! We couldn't just let him go blind. We had to spend some of the chain saw money at the vet. We never bought the chain saw. The news wasn't good. The vet thought that Buhungo had contracted a disease from bird droppings. There was no way to be positive unless we had tests done in another city. Buhungo also had worms. The vet wormed him. He gave Buhungo some antibiotics and sent him home. Maybe the antibiotics would work. The vet said we were lucky that both eyes had not been affected.

Buhungo seemed to be holding his own. He had finished the course of antibiotics. He wasn't any better, but he didn't seem any worse. Then, his other eye became infected. I had to lead him outside to use the bathroom. He couldn't see where he was going. I was distressed. A blind dog was still a live dog though. I'd have to get used to taking care of him. Maybe I could figure out a way to train him so he could get around better.

Buhungo started weakening. He was wheezing. He wouldn't eat. I fed him hotdogs to entice him to eat something, anything. It was probably the worst thing I could have given him. Hotdogs were loaded with salt. His lungs were apparently filling up with fluid and I hadn't realized it. I lead him outside. He didn't want to walk around the yard. I let him lay down on the carport. Maria, our female St. Bernard laid down beside him. She was following him everywhere. Maria was on a death watch. I hadn't known, or didn't want to believe the end was coming. I went out later to check on Buhungo. He was laying on his side with Maria beside him. A puddle of fluid had drained out of his mouth and nose. He was dead. I was saddened to think he had died without one of us there. Maria had been there though.

Maria's sister, Skittles, had been hit and killed by a car before Christmas. Skittles was almost one year old when she died. She had been hit in the early morning hours. We lived in the country so there were not too many cars out at that time. One car was all it took. Maria and Skittles had loved to play in the water that collected in the ditch. After that, Maria learned to stay away from the street and especially not to cross the street to play in the neighbor's ditch. It had been a hard lesson. I swore I'd never get another puppy until we had a fence around our yard. Now we had only Maria left. I hate to admit that I thought this, but it was probably for the best. I know it's cruel, but we couldn't afford to properly take care of three Saint Bernards and at least a dozen cats. We couldn't even take care of ourselves.

About two weeks after Buhungo died I came down with a very severe case of conjunctivitis. I had been to a nurse practitioner at the Christian County Medical Clinic, but the eye drops weren't working. My eye was angry, sore, red, and swollen. I showed up for work with a wet washcloth over my eye. I don't know what I was thinking. I guess I was afraid not to show up for work. The principal saw me and immediately made an appointment for me to see a specialist that day. The doctor said that I had one of the worst cases of conjunctivitis she had ever seen. She questioned me about the eye disease my dog had before it died. She called my vet to see if I could possibly have the same disease. I was given eye drops, Motrin, and sent home. I went to bed immediately.

Maria started following me around the house. Did she think I was dying too? Was I dying? Was I going to go blind? Did I catch the disease from Buhungo? I started to conceive of ways I could manage to work and be productive if I lost my eyesight. I had to work. I had a family to support, blind or not. One week later, I was very much alive. My eyes had cleared up.

My biggest fear was that animal control would come out to our house and see all the cats we had. None of them were spayed or neutered. We couldn't afford it. I searched the Internet for any organizations that would provide free or low cost spaying and neutering. I didn't have any luck. The females kept getting pregnant. No one wanted to adopt cats or kittens. I was frantic. What was I going to do?

I toyed with the thought of dropping them off at the shelter. I didn't want them to be euthanized. They didn't deserve to die just because I couldn't afford to get them fixed. Even if they didn't kill the cats I'd probably get a huge fine or something. I knew I'd be in trouble in some way. Was it legal to have this many cats? The guy across the street had fed about thirty cats at one time. He said he didn't claim any of them as his own. Okay, at least I didn't have thirty cats, but I would if they didn't stop reproducing! On top of this, all the cats were looking thin. I bought some tapeworm medicine at the Big R store and lined up all the cats for a dose. They all got a dose of roundworm medicine as well. To help them get fat, I bought some Nutri-Cal, concentrated calorie gel, for cats and a supply of wet food. This was the best I could do by them for now.

If any of the cats got hurt I had to doctor them myself. There was no money for veterinarians. I got pretty good at patching up cats. I used the same things we'd use on our own cuts and scrapes. Gray Kitty, one of our longhairs, had stuck his front leg through his flea collar. No one had noticed. By the time we noticed him limping, he had a deep cut from the collar rubbing against his fur. The laceration extended all the way from his shoulder to his chest. I removed the collar and cleaned the wound. He really looked like he could have used some stitches. I wasn't about to sew up a cat. This was where my medical expertise ended. I'd be sliced up more than the cat was by the time I got through.

However, I had recently watched a documentary on female circumcision and birthing. It was pretty disturbing stuff. The point is, I had learned from that show that some wounds could be left to heal open, without stitches. It was horrifying that such things could go on in this day and age, but I guess these women survived being left gaping open after giving birth. I found some gauze and some antibacterial lotion. I smeared the lotion on the wound thickly and wrapped Gray Kitty up. I'd check on it every day for signs of infection. If it worked, Gray Kitty would be fine and I would have saved us some money we didn't have to spend in the first place. If it didn't work, well…Within a few days, Gray Kitty was back to normal and healing nicely.

One cat catastrophe that had me worried was Runt Baby. Runt Baby had done something to her front paw. I didn't know if it was broken or what. She wouldn't put any weight on it and the paw was swollen three or four times its original size. Other than her paw she acted fine. I gently washed her paw in water and antibacterial liquid. I didn't immediately see anything wrong with it. Maybe a bee had stung her. The bones didn't feel broken. In any case, I'd see what she was like tomorrow.

Later, we discovered that Runt Baby had somehow managed to rip one of her claws out of position and had made it turn sideways. I couldn't fix this. She had me scared. What if it turned into gangrene? I might have to figure out a way to kill Runt Baby! I didn't own a gun. I didn't think I could kill her even if I did own one. I could run over her with the car. No, no! Killing a cat is probably a criminal offense. I'd be thrown in jail yet. After some time, the paw didn't seem to bother Runt Baby as much. The swelling went down. She was walking on it again. It mostly bothered her in cold weather after that. I felt so guilty. I was a negligent animal owner, but only because I had no money. I'm sure that is no excuse, but I was doing the best I could.

The undercurrent of strife at work had become so unbearable that I couldn't take it any more. I had originally considered resigning over Christmas break, but I talked myself out of it. I had signed a contract to teach for a full school year. Teachers just don't walk out on their students like that. What would my students think? There were some genuinely nice parents and students that would probably be bewildered by such an action on my part. I had to live up to my obligations. It was my duty to go back and make the best of it. After all, my family was depending on me as their main source of income. I returned after Christmas break, but things kept getting worse. Spring break rolled around and I struggled with the idea of jumping ship midstream again. I had no other job to go to. I was the primary breadwinner. My family was counting on me. If I quit now we may indeed, possibly wind up homeless. At this point, living in a cardboard box looked good compared to having to go back to that school for even one more day. Every day I came home more and more irritable from work.

I was sick of being hauled into the principal's office and getting reprimanded every single day over stupid stuff. I was even lectured to because I gave a permission slip to a parent in the wrong way. How can you hand a permission slip to a parent in an incorrect manner you ask? It sounds impossible, right? I had handed the slip to the parent in the hallway before our field trip. I told the parent, after looking at the long list of violations included on the form that, "We wouldn't have any of these problems." I said, "These are good kids." No sooner than I had uttered those few words, I found myself being confronted by the principal again. Now what did I do? This was really getting old. I must be in trouble for something that happened yesterday or several days ago. I had no clue what was going on. The principal stated something to the effect that the reason why the children in this school are good is because they have rules to follow. She made an implication that I was not taking the school rules seriously. Everyone must be totally insane around this place! Judging from my life, I was the only one that truly had a right to be psychotic! Was she having a menopausal moment, or did she just thrive on creating drama and tormenting teachers? I had no idea, but I didn't want to stick around to find out. This was too much.

Another time, I was chewed out for hanging some pictures the children had colored on the wall. I had given coloring sheets to any child that thought they would like to be in band next semester. The kids could pick out the instrument they wanted to play and color it. There was no grade involved. They weren't forced to color one if they didn't want to. We're talking crayons here! Innocent, right? My great sin was posting these pictures on the wall with a title above them. The title read, *New Band Students*. All it took was one parent to freak out and my carcass was summoned to the principal's office again.

I was sent over to my *New Band Students* display to deal with the irate parent. Now, why would a parent be so offended you may ask? Had I mistakenly forgotten to hang up their little darling's artwork? Oh, no! It would be the guillotine for me! Had their child been upset because they wanted to play a flute and had colored a clarinet instead? Perhaps, their baby hadn't colored the picture to the best of their ability. Maybe, the parent wanted a duplicate copy because *obviously* it must be my fault that their child had done a bad job on the first one? The picture didn't look too bad in my opinion. I didn't understand what the problem was. I thought parents liked to see their children's work exhibited. At least, in every other school I had been in this was the norm.

My great sin had been to post the words, *New Band Students*, above the pictures. Evidently, the grievance was that the students had not officially enrolled in band yet. The best I could surmise was that the angry parent hadn't wanted the coloring sheet to obligate her to pay additional fees for band. How ridicules was that? Kids change their minds all the time. I knew that some of the kids would probably not wind up being in band. All I was attempting to do was promote enrollment. Encouraging enrollment was part of my job. Maybe if the students saw the pictures their friends had drawn on the wall, they'd get interested in being in band too. Whatever! I was fed up with the whole thing. I didn't care anymore.

The parent demanded that the picture be removed. She didn't even want the picture her child had colored. The principal ordered that the wording be changed. Fine! I'll change the wording. What was I supposed to say, "Possible New Band Students?" If this was the case, then the Future Farmers of America, a long-standing organization, well known throughout the country, should have to change their club's name to Potential, but not Definite Future Farmers of American! This was so stupid!

I removed all the pictures and the wording. The carefully stenciled, blue letters that I had taken the extra time to cut out, found their way to the nearest trash can. I gave the pictures back to the respective children. The other kids were bewildered and wondered why I was giving their pictures back to them after only a couple of days. I muttered something unintelligible about not being allowed to post them. Now, I'd probably be in trouble for removing all the pictures instead of just the one, or wasting the perfectly reusable stenciled letters. So, kill me!

I found myself trying to avoid the principal in the hallways and not returning calls to parents for fear they were going to launch another unfounded attack. I couldn't handle any more of this. I had wanted to be a music teacher since I was a kid! Why couldn't they just let me teach music without all this garbage? Why did they have to find fault with every little thing? I clearly didn't comprehend the politics of my work environment. Thank God Spring break was coming up.

With two days left before spring break was over, I went to the post office. I bought an express mail envelope. I placed my keys to my office and a short resignation letter inside. Maybe it wasn't the most professional way to quit, but I couldn't bear to look at the principal's face again. In fact, I addressed my resignation to the reverend of the church, not the principal. I did this because I didn't want another baseless accusation made against me. I felt that I couldn't trust the principal not to make up some claim that I never turned my keys in. Perhaps, I was becoming paranoid from working there. I could just see one of the school owned instruments getting stolen. They had been robbed before. Then, the principal would say I never sent in my keys. Therefore, it must be me that ripped it off. A number of scenarios popped into my mind. As soon as the package was sent I realized I should have sent it by certified mail. I wanted a signature that someone received it.

I feared being sued for breach of contract by quitting in the middle of the year. I was apprehensive of some sort of reprisal. I never received any further communication from the school with the exception of a bill for the lunches I had eaten which amounted to about $25.00. I didn't pay it. As little as they paid, the lunches should have been included as a benefit like they were at the Head Start program.

Now, I had more pressing issues. I had just quit my job, my family was in jeopardy of being homeless and/or starving and I had no prospects. I had a part-time job that I had acquired in March to supplement my pathetic income that the school was paying me. I was the director of the Taylorville Park Singers, a children's show choir, but that only brought in $500/month. I had begun a job search back in November when I had originally considered quitting. None of the employers I had sent letters to had called me. I angrily told Jon not to worry. I knew what I was doing! I was determined that I would have another job within twenty-four hours. Unlike Jon, I knew the urgency of our situation and was ready to act. I would do whatever it took to take care of my kids. I told him to inform Burger King that he could have more hours now.

I desperately cruised the want ads. I saw one that caught my eye. I drove to the location and filled out an application. It seemed like a fun work place. There was music playing and flashing party lights. This seemed like just the change I needed. It was time to lighten up after being in that nit-picking, disapproving, fault-finding school environment. Later that evening, I received a phone call to interview the next day. The voice on the phone said, "Hi, this is Sarah. You may not remember me, but you took care of me and my sisters when we were little."

God was on my side again! God was smiling and saying, "Congratulations! I was wondering how long you would put up with that last job. I did everything I could do to get you to quit." The girl I had once baby-sat was now going to hire me. I had held true to my word. I had landed another job within twenty-four hours.

Chapter Seven:
Working on the Wild Side

Are you one of the everything-in-my-life-has-always-been-wonderful Christians? Skip this chapter! It was not meant for your virgin ears!

I was now working as a telemarketer. It wasn't the most sought after of jobs, but you'll do anything when you're desperate and have a family to feed. I do mean *anything*. There were several *entrepreneurs* at the telemarketing center. There were all sorts of illegal businesses that people had on the side. One lady sold bootlegged CDs. Others would sell their food stamps for some cash. For example, if someone didn't have enough money for groceries, the person with the food stamps might sell $50.00 of their stamps for $25.00 in hard cash. Of course, there was always drug dealing going on. I was probably one of the only ones that hadn't been arrested.

One man that worked there was actually mature. He was probably in his forties. I figured he hadn't been arrested for anything and had probably lived a crime-free life. He wasn't crazy like the rest of them. He didn't get in fights. He never even cussed and *everyone* cussed.

(Pent up stress and frustration is often released in one's choice of language.) He wore professional attire whereas, the average male telemarketer wore scraggly jeans and tees. Most of the females barely *wore* clothes. This guy looked like a person that had worked at a high paying office job and had found himself laid off suddenly. He seemed out of his element. I found out later that *Mister Maturity* had been incarcerated as a kiddie sex offender! It was a rowdy and wild place. I saw more insanity there than at any job I had ever had in my life. I also had more fun there than at any job I ever held in my life.

Spring turned into summer. The managers and the boss kept us entertained to be sure. It was more of a party atmosphere than a work environment. My day started at nine in the morning. This was the earliest we were allowed to call people by law. The boss would crank up the stereo full blast with some tunes. The people we were calling could hear all the noise and loud music and often commented on it. Some of the customers, on the other end of the phone, thought we were partying. They weren't too far off. This was not elevator music! It was not relaxing, easy listening, muzak stuff. This was current rap, hip hop and dance hits. We sang. We danced if the music moved us. We batted balloons back and forth to each other. They passed out water-filled yo-yo balls for us to play with. We had crazy dress up days. If we made a lot of sales they would order pizza. We had daily spiffs to earn extra money and prizes for our sales. Sometimes they would give out lottery tickets if we made a sale. Sometimes we got coupons to Subway. We played darts. We played all kinds of games. They brought us cookies. They kept the free coffee and hot chocolate flowing into our veins and often walked up and down the aisles and waited on us as if they were flight attendants. We laughed and cracked jokes from the moment we walked into the building.

The ultimate in hilarity was when we all got together and hired a male stripper to come out for the manager's thirty-ninth birthday. The manager's niece had the idea of getting a "cop" to come and *arrest* her aunt. She knew that her aunt had several outstanding traffic tickets and it might be believable. At any rate, the police were known to make frequent appearances at our workplace. I'm telling you, it was an uncivilized place! So, we pooled our money. Then, the big day arrived. We were checking out everyone that came in the building. At first, we thought maybe she had changed her mind about the cop outfit and the coca-cola man was the stripper. He was built and HOT! He managed to deliver the cokes and escape before the females helped him strip. I wouldn't have put it past them. This place would make Sodom and Gomorrah blush!

Finally, right at quitting time we saw a cop, THE COP! He wasn't as good looking as the coke man, but we didn't care. We were ready for some beefcake! I told my Bear what we had planned at work for today so he showed up and sort of hung out by the time clock to see what would happen. Mister cop came in and pretended that our manager was in trouble for her unpaid tickets. She caught on quickly. She was smiling from ear to ear and loving every minute of it. Cop man flipped on his portable ghetto blaster and preceded to gyrate, rotate, shimmy, shake, and shudder his way around the room. In the beginning he was fully clothed. He did some highly charged, sexually explicit pelvic thrusts. He rubbed himself all over our full-figured, yet still attractive, manager. She encouraged it and participated wholly. He sat in her lap trembling as he performed a sensual lap dance. Then, he turned around to face the crowd of rowdy women. After strategically placing a can of silly string in front of his *salami*, he began to spray it straight up, toward the ceiling. This was the first *ejaculation*. Then he started to remove his uniform, one piece at a time. Underneath it he wore only a black thong. He kept his shoes on. He was very athletic and flexible. The manager laid down on the floor. He got on top of her and quivered faster than I thought was humanly possible. He seriously reminded me of when our rabbits had mated. I was wondering if he actually *did it* that fast in private, outside of performing. He didn't actually touch her, but remained within a few inches of her while he carried out the simulated sex act. Now, he pulled out a can of whipped cream, calculatingly positioned it next to his penis, and while standing over her, squirted it into her mouth. The performance went on for about twenty minutes while all of the women unashamedly screamed and cheered him on. My husband, blushing, left after a few minutes. This was by far the best time I had ever had at a place of employment.

Our cross-dressing co-worker was a riot too. We were in a suburb of Springfield, Illinois. This was not Chicago. People around here are not used to seeing men wearing dresses and makeup. If it was shameful, indecent, offensive, shocking, criminal or should otherwise be on the Jerry Springer show, we had it at the telemarketing center. I was sitting outside with the smokers at the picnic table, trying to avoid their toxic emissions, when another co-worker came over and asked, "Have you seen the cross dresser yet"? Now this was something I had to see! He-she was here, at a place of employment, dressed like a woman? You can't dress like that on the job can you? I decided to take a little stroll inside to see what I could see. There it was. She-he, whatever it was, had on a mini skirt, women's sandals, women's jewelry, nail polish and makeup. Its dyed, maroonish-colored hair was tied back in a ponytail and it had a pair of titties, size B cup. Were they implants or a stuffed bra? My best friend offered to grab a hold on them and pinch them to see if they were real or not. I just about died. She never did actually grab them. Thank God!

The mini skirt sure was flat against his legs. I started to wonder if he had had that part of his anatomy removed or altered in some way as well because if he still had it, it wasn't showing. There should have been some kind of a bulge there. The same friend offered to grab that too. I begged her not to. She didn't. It was impossible to concentrate on my phone calls with him-her, *It*, in the room. I stared at this mutant and wondered if it would use the male or the female bathroom. The females didn't want to share a restroom with this creature. The males didn't want this man-woman thing in their restroom either. The boss finally assigned a totally different restroom to this new employee.

It amazed me that he loved to wear dresses, panty hose and heels. Real women tend to hate panty hose, and heels, they are so uncomfortable. After the initial shock value had worn off some, we learned that he was married to a woman and had kids. I thought he was gay. Was he straight? No way, couldn't be! He and his wife actually shared clothes. Maybe they were both bi? He was a nice enough individual once you talked to him, but I still couldn't help, but stare at this peculiarity and wonder. I told my Bear that he could count on certain divorce if I ever find him trying on my clothes. It was beyond me how any woman could put up with her man wanting to be a woman.

I knew this place had lost any hope of professionalism when I witnessed a co-worker sorting through his marijuana on top of his desk, in plain sight! Initially, I hadn't concerned myself with what he was doing. Unlike my younger co-worker, I had been preoccupied with interrupting the American public's peace and serenity in order to badger them into buying a vacation package to Branson. I had, evidently, made some sudden move that startled my twenty-something friend. I wondered what his problem was.

He told me, "I thought the manager had seen me with *it*".

"With what?"

He showed me his stash. "You are kidding me right? You mean to tell me you brought your weed in here?"

"Sssshhh," he whispered.

"I am not believing that you actually brought weed in here," I restated.

"Smell it," he dared.

I smelled the dried up herb he had on his desk. "It smells like oregano," I teased.

"It's not oregano," he corrected, as if I didn't believe it was actually pot.

He went back to sorting and picking out the seeds.

Everyone knew that you buy, sell, and do drugs in the parking lot, not inside! He was stupid to bring it inside. If he got caught it wasn't going to be my problem, but now it was impossible for me to get up and take a break. If I left to go to the bathroom, and then the boss busted him out while I was gone, he'd blame me for ratting on him. I wasn't scared of him causing me any physical harm. It wasn't like that. I just didn't want him to think that I was a snitch if he got in trouble.

Having the police out was almost a daily event. They called the police whenever they fired someone. They did this because a few people they fired had refused to leave. Instead, they wanted to stick around and fight about it. This was usually just a heated verbal exchange. However, around this place it could have easily escalated into violence.

The police were kept busy separating the many fights that broke out among the employees. I honestly enjoyed watching the frequent fights. I learned to be careful about what you say or you might be yanked into the battle too! One day, I was outside at the picnic table when I heard a harsh exchange of words. A female employee had just hurled an angry oral assault at another female employee. Yes, perfect, a little lunch time entertainment was brewing! Gleefully, I sat up and paid attention. Obviously, the words had not done sufficient damage to the intended party so the aggressor picked up a half empty bottle of Pepsi. Oh, *now* this was getting better. Unbridled hostility is always so much fun! The instigating female launched the Pepsi as hard as possible in the direction of the victim. She evidently needed more pitching practice. The projectile grazed an innocent, female bystander and slammed violently into the side of the building with a loud thud! Now, three women were in this little skirmish!

"Watch out Bitch", she screamed as the flying Pepsi hit her.

She gave the assailant an enraged look and put her purse down on the sidewalk prepared to *get it on*. Another co-worker, Mr. Maturity, the pervert, tried to counsel her that it wasn't worth it.

"What did you call me, Bitch?!," the attacker questioned as she pushed her way through the gathering crowd.

"I called you a 'Bitch', BITCH!," she yelled!

I don't know what the original dispute was about, but by this time the first target had fled. What a pity! Two against one would have been more exciting and there would have been a much greater chance of some real bloodshed. Miss Attacker landed a punch to Miss Bystander's shoulder. Miss Bystander countered with several cat scratches and slaps. I smiled. Miss Attacker retaliated with several slaps and scratches of her own. Two male employees ran out and grabbed the females around their waists, pulling them apart. Man! This was just getting good! Why couldn't they have waited just a few seconds more? I really wanted to see this fight go to the ground. I didn't even get to witness any kicking, hair pulling or biting yet! What a let down! The police showed up immediately. My dinner theatre show was over. Time to go back to work.

On occasion, the police came by on their own just looking for people. The police knew that there were a lot of people of ill repute hired there. If they got lucky they might find someone on their "wanted" list. I was told that as long as they didn't have any weapons charges they were usually hired. Apparently, they had hired someone once that had weapons charges against him. This criminally minded individual got peeved over something at work one day. He threatened to come back the next day and kill everyone. Boss lady said she didn't take any chances because this guy was from East St. Louis, an area known for its high crime rate. She had the police there when she opened the building. The would be assassin never showed.

Just think, these depraved people were calling *your* house! We were all smooth talkers. If you weren't a silver-tongued slicker you became one real fast or you wouldn't have a job there anymore. It was just part of the business to be able to talk people into buying trips to Branson that they didn't need and hadn't necessarily considered. Some people had never even heard of Branson, Missouri and we *still* sold them on the idea of going! You sell or you're out of a job was the battle cry! We'd tell the customer just about anything they wanted to hear to make the sale. If you cussed us out we might very well return fire. We'd definitely crack jokes to our co-workers about you and your self-important attitude when we hung up. Every day, consumers willingly gave us their credit card numbers and personal banking information. I'm sure this would not have been the case if Mr. and Mrs. Joe Blow customer would have seen the person they were talking to. Dr. Bigshot Bazillionaire would probably have never given the time of day to a cross dresser, but here they were giving him their credit card number?! Dr. Bigshot and Mr. J. Blow were just asking for a case of identity theft! What bizarre twist of fate had landed me here? I was a recent college graduate. Is this the best I could do for myself? I guess so.

Any respectable neighborhood would not have put up with us during the summer of 2003. If our lives were a reality show we would have been voted out of the neighborhood. This was the summer that we did not cut our grass at all! We didn't have a riding lawn mower, not even a push mower. We have four and a half acres and not a single blade of grass was cut all summer! We weren't on strike. We weren't trying to restore the natural environment. It wasn't about creating a wildlife habitat. We hadn't turned into flower children. We hadn't even started a cult! We weren't being lazy either. We just didn't have the money to buy a mower! Yes, I know that cheapie push mowers only cost about a hundred bucks. I just didn't have it!

Little Jon measured a dandelion that grew to be almost four feet tall that year! We also had some weeds that closely resembled marijuana, only with fatter leaves, that grew to be over fifteen feet tall! They had sturdy stalks, which came in handy when I sprained my right calf muscle. Very, OUCH! No, I didn't smoke them for pain relief! However, it might have worked. I'm sure it must have been in the same plant family. We didn't have any medical insurance and no money to see a doctor so we did what we had to do. Little Jon set to work and wrapped three big stalks together with duct tape. He cut some shorter pieces of stalk for the armrest and covered them with a pillowcase. I was still working at the telemarketing center at this time. They knew I lived out in the country and laughed when they saw me hobbling in on a *Beverly Hillbillies* crutch. I told them my kid made it for me. They wanted to know what it was made of. I almost didn't make it home with that crutch! They were ready to cut it up and smoke it! I had many offers to cut my grass after that. I turned down all their offers. It would be my luck they would find the real thing growing somewhere on my property. I had heard that the previous owners of our house sold drugs. I don't know about that, but I did find a roach clip in one of the air vents when we first moved in. I didn't want to go to jail! Then again, at least in prison you have food, water, heat, air conditioning, cable TV, access to a free education, an exercise area and can see a doctor if you sprain your *friggin* leg! Prison, and all its benefits, sounded pretty good about right now! The prisoners had everything we didn't have!

It was August 2003. Our income was pathetic. My income had fallen drastically due to the economy and waning sales. We were about to lose our home for the second time.

I fully understood that adults stand or fall on their own two feet. I understood that to go crawling for help once you become an adult is shameful and degrading. Begging for help makes you less than an adult. I also understood that I was not Fran's daughter and she was in absolutely no way obliged to help me save my house. In her eyes I was probably just some pitiful, straggly orphan her son had brought home over a decade ago. Furthermore, it wasn't her fault that Jon and I had two kids that we now, if truth be told, couldn't really support. She had no responsibility to help me. I also understand that some people honestly cannot help because they do not have the resources to do so. On the other hand, I recognize that some people do have the means.

It was obvious that Jon's mother didn't want us to live in Illinois. She wanted us to be in Texas near her. She had offered to let us live in her home in Big Spring last August, when we were facing homelessness then. If we had moved into her home we'd, more than likely, be thrown out by the rest of Jon's family as soon as she died. I knew how these kinds of things turn out from experience. We would then be without a roof over our heads in poverty stricken Big Spring, where we knew no one.

Jon's mom had even offered to buy a house for us where she currently lived. She absolutely refused to help us save our home in Illinois with the excuse that she didn't have any money to help us with. She would buy a house and pay for our moving costs, but couldn't help us with a couple of late house payments because she couldn't afford it? Buying a house was a most generous offer, but at what cost?

Somewhere along the line, the words "tough love" and "enabling" started appearing. Helping your adult children out financially wasn't a good thing. Therefore, one must practice tough love, which means, not helping at all. To help people would mean you were enabling them. Enabling them to do what? Have a place to live? How is this a bad thing? Obviously there was a huge chasm between our culture of poverty and whatever his family's cultural laws dictated.

Now I can see how a parent wouldn't lend financial support to a drug addict or an alcoholic. They'd just go buy drugs or have another beer. I can even understand how a parent wouldn't let an adult child that refused to work have money for rent. If they lost their apartment and had to live on the streets, oh well, as long as there were no grandchildren involved that had to suffer; however, I was working. Wanting a place for my kids to live wasn't quite the same as drinking, doping or being lazy.

Something about Fran's favorite motto, "He who has the money makes the rules", bothered me immensely. Fran insisted that we move "home" to Texas. She didn't realize that Illinois *was* our home. She said she hadn't seen us in a long time. Even when we had lived in Texas she rarely visited us. We hadn't had the money to drive to St. Louis, which was just two hours away, for a day trip to Six Flags in years. We sure didn't have the money to drive half way across the country to visit her. Fran said she didn't know what we needed with us being so far away. If we tried to tell her about all the things that were going on in our lives she would get overwhelmed and hang the phone up. No, Fran really didn't want to hear the whole story. She just thought she did. She couldn't handle it. Fran was from a different time and a different world. In her United States, a place that really existed I'm told, only people too lazy to work were this destitute. I was working my butt off, but somehow work just didn't mean a whole lot in my world.

In an effort to help Jon's family understand our plight, I had started writing a monthly newsletter. One letter a year at Christmas just didn't cut it. We had more trauma in one week than most families experience in a lifetime. After about my third such newsletter, one of Jon's relative's basically told me I was a liar and that I was exaggerating. What kind of demented, freak of a person lies about these sorts of things? Did they really think I just sat around dreaming up these horrible events? I quit writing to his family. It was pointless.

Sara and Little Jon had donated all their money last year to save our house. I had not been able to pay them back since. The kids had nothing. I had nothing. Jon had nothing. We had tried to refinance our house in June, just two months earlier, when Jon had lost his job at Burger King. Jon had been too scared to call in and tell Burger King that he wasn't going to be at work and they fired him. What was Jon thinking?! I had only insisted that Jon go to a job fair and try to find a better paying job. I shouldn't have had to nag Jon to look for better employment in the first place! I sure hadn't insisted that he act irresponsibly and just not show up for work with no reason. Tell them your sick! Say your car broke down! Come up with any excuse, but don't just *not* show up! Why did I even have to go over such clear-cut things with him?! It was infuriating!

The Hardees, in Chatham, hired him a few weeks later, but Jon had far fewer hours at Hardees than he had had at Burger King. Coupled with having fewer hours, Jon was falling asleep on the job again. He fell asleep standing up while breading the chicken. He also forgot to get the biscuits out of the oven and they burned. Who knows how long this job would last? We had wanted to refinance our house so we could lower our payments by a couple hundred dollars a month. This way the payments wouldn't be such an impossible burden to us every month. The bank wouldn't work with us. Our overall credit was bad due to the fact we hadn't been able to keep up with the credit cards when I was in college. Our mortgage payments had been late too often. Wait! Jon had a coin collection somewhere. Sara tore through her Daddy's things to find the coins that could possibly save our lives and our house. Jon didn't want to part with his coin collection.

"Maybe if you had worked we wouldn't have to do this." I glared.

"I have been working!"

"You haven't worked professionally in years!"

"A lot of those coins are old!"

"Good, they'll be worth something then!"

"I was saving them."

"Saving them for what? People save things like this for emergencies! This is an emergency!"

"I don't want to sell the coins," Jon growled.

"Would you rather be homeless?"

"What's this? Where did this come from?"

Sara came into the living room with a wad of rolled up bills. She took the rubber band off and started counting. "One hundred, two hundred, two hundred twenty, one, two, three…" she counted.

Little Jon had grabbed half the bills and was doing his own counting.

"How much do you have?"

"I don't know yet," Little Jon stated. "Now I lost count. You messed me up."

"Give me what you have. Let's count it all together."

When the counting was done there was just enough to save the house for the second time. We were saved! Now all eyes stared threateningly at Big Jon.

"Where did all this money come from?"

"I've been saving it. It's special!"

"What is so special about it? Money is money!"

"Some of these are two dollar bills and one dollar bills that are older. Some of them go back to 1934."

"This one is a 1974 dollar bill. This is a 1997! Now tell me what is so special about this!"

I waved the one dollar bill in the air.

"Nothing, you can go ahead and use it."

"When were you going to tell us about it, after we were on the streets?" I was indignant.

"This pisses me off that you were hiding money from us when we need it so desperately! Where did you get all these bills anyway?"

"I collected them when I worked the drive through window at the Burger King."

"You traded your money you had in your pocket for this?"

"Yes."

"Money is too precious to be playing games with it like this. This money could have bought groceries or school supplies," I was outraged.

"Me and Little Jon gave all our money to Mommy last summer and you had this in your closet? We would still have our money if you would have used this!" Sara was fuming and rightfully so.

"I would have had to use your money this time though," I told Sara.

"It doesn't matter. He should have used his money first and not taken mine and Little Jon's. He is supposed to be taking care of me and Little Jon. You are the parents. We've had to go without food and water and heat!"

"I've done the best that I could. I went to school double full-time for four and a half years. Then I worked two and three jobs at a time trying to keep a roof over your head and food in your mouth," I retorted.

"We got our food from the food pantries," Sara pointed out.

"And I was the one who found the food pantries and went to them. I had to do whatever it took and if that meant going to a food pantry then that's what I did."

"But he didn't do anything! He let us starve!"

As summer turned into fall, our water supply was drying up. We had practically no water at all. Sara had managed to get into some poison ivy and hadn't been able to shower it off! She was less than happy. Our sales at the telemarketing center were also drying up. Then the economy bottomed out and no one wanted to buy vacation packages to Branson any more. They especially didn't want to give out their personal banking information over the phone and who would blame them? There were warnings on the television and radio about us evil telemarketers. There were too many scams out there to trust anyone and that made it hard for us. Along with this, the national, *Do Not Call List*, was put into effect. Several potential customers were automatically removed from our calling lists. Several people who thought they should have been removed got really freakoid when we called them. One man threatened to "cut off my tits" if I ever called him again! I should have come up with an equally nasty counter reply, but I was too stunned. Hindsight is truly 20/20. If I had it to do over again I would've told him that, "I'd love to likewise, remove his pathetically undersized dick with a pair of dull, rusty scissors and run it down the garbage disposal!" That way, I'd be sure that he couldn't go running to the emergency room, penis in hand, wanting them to sew it back on. As small as it probably was, it would require microscopic surgery at that!

Another lady wanted the name and address of my company so she could sue me and get her $10,000, which was the fine if telemarketers harassed you. I gave her the name of my company and talked good-naturedly to her for several minutes. She was actually a very pleasant lady. I figured even if she did sue me my life couldn't get much worse. I didn't have ten grand. Besides, you can't really sue people who don't have any money because you'll never collect. She didn't want to ruin anyone's life. She just wanted to be able to have some money so she could live hers. I understood completely. I gave her my boss's name, the address in Branson and wished her luck, *winning the lottery,* as it were. Suing people had become a national past time and I can only imagine why. Somewhere along the line when legitimate employment had failed to provide a living wage, people had turned to outrageous lawsuits as one means of survival. People were suing restaurants for making them fat?! Someone else sued a restaurant because they spilled coffee on them self and got burnt! Lawsuits, identity theft and drug dealing, that's where the American entrepreneurial spirit had gone.

All this amusement was not meant to endure forever. My commissions had dropped to non-existent. We were paid $7.00 to $10.00 an hour depending on how many vacation packages we sold. I hadn't sold any packages so I was making $7.00 an hour with no extra commission. My hours were 9:00 a.m. until 2:30 p.m. with a half hour break. I was making $35.00 a day. A family of four cannot live on $35.00 a day!

The Chevy Lumina had been going through radiator fluid faster than a cornstalk sucks up rain in an Illinois drought. Radiator fluid got to be too expensive so we took to filling her up with plain water. Thirty-five dollars a day wasn't going to buy radiator fluid much less pay for any car repairs. We carried a jug or two of water in the trunk at all times.

The Lumina decided to die in traffic on me outside the power plant in Springfield one hot day. My extra jug of water was empty. I'd have to hike across the busy intersection, in a dress no less, and see if the power plant would let me have a gallon of water. Several cars stopped and asked if I needed to use their cell phone to call for help. I had no one to help me. I could call home, but Jon couldn't come and get me. This was our only car. We really didn't have any close friends to ask. The in-laws lived in different states. This was usually a good thing. Right now I would have killed for a brother, dad, or an uncle to come rescue me. My father was dead. I never really had an uncle or a brother. I had met my half brother once, at my father's funeral. I had never met any of my mother's brothers. I wasn't quite sure of their names or where they lived to tell the truth. I had to deal with this on my own, no different than anything else I suppose. I politely told the motorists that I didn't have anyone to call.

The course dried grass scraped at my bare legs as I walked along the ditch. I came up to the guard booth at the plant. The security officer let me in. This was a miracle in itself, especially after the September 11th terrorist attacks. Everyone, including power plants, was on high alert for terrorists. I guess I didn't fit the terrorist profile. I wasn't male or from the Middle East. I was shown to an employee break room and filled my water jug. I started to walk back to the car. I popped the hood and filled the radiator. It would take a few minutes before the car would start again, *if* it started again. It had to cool first. This problem had been going on for awhile now. After a few minutes the car started and I made it the rest of the way home.

One day while I was at work the car died completely. Jon called to tell me the bad news.

"Try to get the truck started," I pleaded. "Okay, I'll see if I can get it running," Jon said.

I had been working the night shift. I was stranded at work, thirty miles from home, with no way home. No one at work lived out my direction. I was starting to see the need for close friendships, of which I had none currently. I begged a guy that lived in Taylorville if he'd go out of his way a few miles so I could get home. He said, "When my Mom comes to pick me up I'll ask her."

If his Mom wouldn't take me home I had two choices. I could start walking the thirty miles, in the dark, alone, or I would have to sleep outside somewhere near work until morning. If I spent the night outside, at least I'd be here tomorrow morning for my shift. It might be a little chilly being outside all night, but I'd survive. Then, after my shift tomorrow I'd have all afternoon to walk the thirty miles to my house and at least it would be daylight. I'd probably have a better chance to get someone to take me home tomorrow afternoon.

Meanwhile, Big Jon was at home feverishly trying to resurrect the 1974 Ford pickup truck. It hadn't run in quite some time. Jon poured gas down the carburetor in a last effort to make the truck live. He put the key into the ignition switch and turned it. The engine burst into searing flames which melted and charred various engine parts. Jon threw dirt and rocks on the engine to extinguish the fire. That truck wasn't going

SPREAD THE PEANUT BUTTER THIN!

to go anywhere, ever again. By the grace of God and all his angels I was able to hitch a ride home with the guy that lived in Taylorville. His Mom wouldn't accept any money for gas. This was a good thing because I had no idea how I'd ever find a way to work from now on. I might be looking at my last little bit of money I would have for a very long time.

We had no money to get another car. Perhaps if I went to that car lot that advertised, "Your job is your credit", they'd work with me. Maybe they could help me get a loan for a cheap car. First, I'd have to find a way over to their car lot. With any luck, if I called one of their salesmen in the morning they would come and pick me up at my house and take me to the lot. I might be able to make some small payments on an old used car. I knew in my inner being that I didn't stand a chance of getting financed for a even the cheapest of cars. My income wasn't even enough to finance my family's grocery bill, who was I trying to fool?

The next day I called in to work and said I couldn't make it. I didn't have a way to get there. Over the next few days I bummed a ride to my job with an acquaintance we knew that lived in Rochester. I paid him twenty dollars a week. This was a fortune considering my dismal paychecks. A few days, he wasn't able to take me to work. I had to miss work on those days. Missing work meant losing out on that day's pay. Without each and every day's wages my family was really suffering. I was lucky that I worked in a place where the boss wasn't too picky on attendance. Otherwise, I probably would have been fired. At least I worked when I was there, unlike some of my co-workers.

At this point, I probably should have had a nervous breakdown. Unfortunately, nervous breakdowns are reserved for the select few that have insurance, a sustainable second income in the family, are rich, famous, or those that are not the primary breadwinner. Since I did not qualify on any of those conditions, I sucked it up and went on autopilot hoping the rapture would come soon, like in the next five minutes. If nothing else, maybe I'd be killed in an accident or die of natural causes. When trying to survive becomes too hard, the ultimate certainty of eventual death is a sweet comfort to those living in extreme poverty.

After nearly two weeks of not having a car I absolutely had to go to the grocery store for a scant few things. We couldn't afford much. I also had to pay my phone and electric bills. We had quit using a checking account about two years ago so all our bills were paid in person by money order. We had never had enough money in our checking account to make it worthwhile and we were always overdrawn. I called swap shop. Swap shop is a very useful little call-in radio show based in Taylorville on WTIM, 93.7 FM. You can advertise anything you have to buy, sell, trade, give away, or if you need a service done. I needed a ride into town. There are no busses or taxis were we live out in the boonies, fifteen miles from Taylorville. For that matter, there were no taxis or busses *in* Taylorville. Within minutes, I had several calls. A female voice in distress, broadcast across the airwaves, tends to bring out quite a few responses from would be knights. A few minutes later my chariot had arrived. A bubba in a pick-up truck drove up my driveway. I wasn't about to get in a truck with someone I didn't know by myself. I made Jon come with me. Bubba took us to the bank to pay the electric bill. Then we went to the phone company. Then we were off to the grocery store. We went home and paid him twenty bucks for his time and gas. Would the ride have been free had I been single, skinnier, and younger?

Depression, starvation, homelessness, hopelessness, anger, frustration, and lack of basic necessities loomed over me like a foreboding, demonic presence. Nevertheless, I showed up for work ever day that I could get a ride. I wasn't very "Christian" in my language, actions, or thoughts anymore. Even so, one of the new guys at work still noticed that I was a Christian. How in the world did he notice that? Did I bring a Bible to work? No. Did I witness or even mention God at work? No. If I did mention God at work it was probably to take his name in vain. I have no idea how the newbie knew I was a Christian. All I was doing was walking along the sidewalk outside the building and he came up to me. "I can tell you are different than the rest of them. You're a Christian, aren't you?"

What the heck? Was I glowing or what? I was so shocked by his question that I don't remember my answer. I don't remember his name, but I wondered if he was an angel. Maybe he was an angel sent to send me a message that God still considers me one of His own, even through all of this never ending nightmare.

We called up Jon's mom and begged for help. If she wouldn't help us get a car we'd have to figure something else out. Without a car I couldn't get to work. Without a job we were facing homelessness and starvation, again. We had no savings to buy a car outright. Jon's mom didn't want to help us buy another car. She had bought the Lumina for us just five years earlier. The Lumina had 200,000 miles on it when it had died. That's a good life span for any car. We had tried to keep it alive, but that was an impossible task considering we couldn't afford to repair anything. We barely were able to pay for the insurance and oil changes. Neither Jon nor myself knew anything about fixing cars. Jon's mom hadn't wanted to pay for repairs. It wasn't her responsibility to do so, after all. In the end, we had no choice, but to drive it until it died.

I don't know why, but Jon's mom had a change of heart. God still works miracles! Jon's sister Rhonda was sent to Springfield to scout out our situation. We hadn't been lying. We really didn't have a car. I really couldn't get to my job. Rhonda spent all day in Springfield trying to find the least expensive, new car possible. Fran stayed at her home. Sara and I weren't on very good terms with Fran. Together, Fran and Rhonda decided on a new, 2003, Hyundai Accent. Jon and I didn't have any input really. We were beggars so we didn't have the right to be picky.

The car would have an automatic transmission. Sara couldn't drive a stick, but that was okay. I didn't allow her to drive the family car at all. I couldn't afford for her to be in a wreck. I couldn't afford the deductible or any repairs that it might need should that happen. I obviously couldn't afford to replace the car if Sara totaled it. As soon as Sara had turned sixteen she had whined about wanting a driver's license. I suppose it is a natural rite of passage to want a driver's license. I had succumbed to her adolescent whining and let her get the license with the understanding that she would never drive the car. She didn't seem to mind. Having the small, plastic card with her picture on it was a status symbol that most teens had and she desperately wanted one. It was a big mistake on my part. I didn't know my insurance would double even if I never allowed her to drive! We carried liability only, but that was a fortune for us.

The Accent would not have air-conditioning. Rhonda was trying to cut costs wherever she could. Rhonda asked if no air-conditioning was ok with me. What could I say? I needed a way to get to work. Jon told me that Rhonda had asked the dealership if the car could be delivered without a radio, but radios came standard with all the vehicles. Jon's mom often said, "I have the money so, I make all the rules." My Bible reads, "For everyone to whom much is given, from him much will be required," Luke 12:48, NKJV. I never read anything in my Bible about lording over people because you have more money than they do. Rhonda tried to assure me that Jon's mother loved us or she would not have given us such an expensive gift like this. The total amount of the car was around $10,000, including the insurance that was necessary to drive it off the lot. Two days later, Rhonda was on her way home and we had a tiny, green, Hyundai hatchback in our driveway. We were appreciative.

With Big Jon weighing over 250 pounds and Little Jon being over six feet tall and more than 200 pounds himself, the car fit the four of us more like an amusement park ride. You know, the kind that straps you in so tight that you can't move an inch in any direction. It rode low to the ground. It wasn't very good on ice and snow, which there is a lot of in Illinois. Little Jon looked like a contortionist trying to squeeze his body into the little box of a car. Big Jon referred to it as our *street legal go-cart.*

Sara was scared to ride in the back seat. The trunk, if you could call it that, was all of maybe a foot long. A rear end collision would be disastrous if not fatal to the back seat passengers. There were no doors for the backseat passengers and only two tiny windows, that didn't open, on each side. She had a problem with claustrophobia and feared being in a crash and not being able to escape. I didn't particularly cherish the thought of being trapped in the back seat while the teeny car burned, in an upside down position, half way submerged in a creek, on some remotely traveled country road either. Sara got over it, but it took some time. The most important thing was, I could go to work again! My family would survive, maybe.

God had performed another miracle on our behalf. The Hyundai, I named Pickle, was just what we needed as far as gas money was concerned. The car was a compact and would be cheap on gas. Gasoline was our second biggest expense after the house payment. Food should have been any family's second largest expense, but we didn't buy food. We begged for that!

At work, the big shot managers from Branson were flying to Springfield to meet with all of us. The boss lady told us to dress up for the occasion. Our manager and the boss lady had no idea what the reason was for their visit. We thought they were going to tell us about our new location we had heard rumors of. We clocked in and waited for the meeting. Big boss man basically told us that due to declining sales, the office would be closed immediately. There would be no severance pay, of course. It came as a complete surprise to everyone. The police arrived as the boss man was finishing his speech. Boss man knew what kind of a crowd this was and had taken preventative measures and called the police before he told us the news. Tempers flared, but no violence erupted. We were all laid off without warning in October of 2003. I had enjoyed six months of outrageously, insane employment. I would not be afforded this type of lunacy again.

I didn't know what to do. Raw fear and panic set in. Jon had been fired from the night shift at the telemarketing center a few weeks previous to the layoff for his inability to produce sales. My second job, as the Taylorville Park Singers director, was seasonal only. When August had rolled around my pay abruptly ended from the choir job. All Jon had was a part time job at Hardees at this point. It wasn't enough! Sometimes he only got three or four hours for the entire week! He was paid barely above minimum wage. Our income would now total around one hundred dollars a month! We couldn't survive! The game was over and I had lost!

The increasing certainty of homelessness was pressing down around me. Where would we go to live? Are there any shelters around here that take families and for how long? What would we do when we had exhausted our time at the shelter and I still didn't have a job? Where would the kids be going to school? The very meager income I had been making was being taken away from me. I figured it would take at least three months for them to foreclose on the house. We'd be living in a house for the next three months without electricity or a phone because I knew I wouldn't have the money for that now. If I don't have a phone how will I find another job? If we don't have electricity we won't have water because our water runs off an electric pump! I was the primary breadwinner of the family. It felt like I had just been given a death sentence. My whole family was on death row. We had three months before the absolute bottom fell out. Jon had just dropped me off at work and wouldn't even be home to receive my call. I asked my friend for a ride to Taylorville. I figured if I could make it to Taylorville I could find some way home from there. Living in the country has one disadvantage. Finding a ride to work or back home again is almost impossible. We numbly started toward the exit. I paused in the doorway. I felt that I couldn't leave without communicating my thoughts on this matter. I turned and yelled, "Hey, boss man! Go fuck yourself!" I shot the finger.

The long ride to Taylorville via Pawnee and Kincaid was punctuated with a great deal of flamboyant language. In Kincaid we stopped off at my friend's trailer to inform her husband of the current events before going to the unemployment office in Taylorville. The trailer was filled with thick cigarette smoke. This was a great disadvantage to my asthma and I was glad when we left. Upon our arrival in Taylorville I had her drop me off at the unemployment office and we said our goodbyes. She didn't go in with me. I waved and turned to the door. Of course, the office was closed. Was it ever open? Now, I was left without a ride and nowhere to go. I had no money so trying to call Jon from a payphone was not an option. It was freezing outside and I hadn't brought a coat. Not only that, but I was wearing dress clothes. Great! The high school were Sara attended was a few blocks away. I started walking. At least the high school would be warm. I could call home from there. If Jon wasn't home, maybe the school would let me ride the school bus home this afternoon. My mind was spinning with anxiety.

I wandered in to the office of the high school. This was an

emergency. I asked to use the phone. I didn't have any money saved up to be able to move. We didn't even have a credit card to be able to rent a U-Haul truck with! There was no way I could afford first and last months rent on an apartment somewhere. Then there were utility hook ups, water, phone, electricity and deposits. I'd have to give away my St. Bernard, Maria! They don't allow pets in homeless shelters. We'd have to find homes for all the cats, the rabbit and the chickens. Maybe I would finally have to admit defeat and move in to my mother-in-law's old house. Jon answered the phone. I told him to come get me and that we were "fucked." I didn't care who had heard me. I had the secretary summon Sara to the office.

Sara walked into the office and saw me there. I didn't have to tell her we were in major trouble. She knew. I explained what was going on. Sara produced her last paycheck that she had received from her part time job. To top it all off, Sara had quit her job just a few days before because her boss had cheated her out of some of the pay she had earned. Sara's paycheck was just enough to keep the phone on for one more month.

Jon arrived. Sara left school early with us. How could she concentrate on schoolwork when her very survival was again in question? This, unfortunately, wasn't the first time we had faced crushing, overwhelming devastation. I toyed with picking up Little Jon at the middle school. No, I've already disrupted Sara's schooling today. I'd leave Little Jon at school. He could finish the school day without this undue stress. He would find out soon enough. Besides, Little Jon was not legal working age like Sara and there was nothing he could do to help the situation. Major unknowns faced us. Was it too much to ask for a little security and stability in my life? How come everything always had to be so hard? What did I do to deserve this? What sin had I committed? God must hate me! I don't believe in reincarnation, but if there is such a thing I must have been one of the staff at a Nazi death camp in a former life. I was probably the one directly responsible for gassing thousands of innocent infants and children. Maybe I had been Jeffery Dahmer in a previous life to justify all this misery! No wait, I couldn't have been reincarnated as Mr. Dahmer. He wasn't dead when

I had been born. We drove around Taylorville in distress, picking up job applications at every store.

The next morning, I headed into Springfield to file for unemployment. I was told I would receive just slightly over $1000.00 a month. Whew! I could now breathe easier. The telemarketing job had diminished in pay until I was only bringing home about $500.00 a month before they shut us down. We wouldn't have been able to live on that anyway so it was a good thing I had been laid off. I'd be doubling my income by being on unemployment. Our situation was dire, but we would have to subsist until I could figure something out.

With this minuscule income we were now able to get food stamps for the first time! Until recently, the state had considered the value of your car in determining eligibility for food stamps. If you had more than $2,000.00 in assets you were ineligible for food stamps. Our cars have always had a blue book value of $2000.00, or more, so we had always done without food. We would now start receiving slightly under $500.00 per month in food stamps! This monthly amount would dwindle down to about $200 per month soon enough, but this was still an enormous difference from the $25.00 to $50.00 a month we averaged on groceries currently. Later, this amount would be greatly reduced, but for now we could eat like Americans again!

Gone were the old, multi-colored, paper, food stamps in different denominations. The state of Illinois now used what looked like a debit card. We could eat! We could go to the grocery store and actually *choose* what we wanted to eat, instead of totally relying on handouts from the food pantries. Illinois Link Card in hand, we tried to make out a grocery list. It had been a long time since we had been to a real grocery store. We needed everything, but we didn't know what they sold anymore. I'm sure there were many new products we hadn't seen or heard about. It felt as if we had won the lottery. We were tremendously high-spirited as we entered our first real grocery store in years! We were there with intent to buy! I couldn't believe it! We were giddy with anticipation. We flew down each aisle admiring the food. There was so much to choose from! How could we choose? We could have easily spent all the money on our Link Card right then, but it had to last all month. I coached the kids not to act too excited or someone might think we were crazy. Medicaid had picked us back up so we were able to go to a doctor and get medicines again, too. I had spent the last four months without my diabetic meds! I hadn't been able to eat much of anything during the last four months. A pack of ramen noodles, which was mostly what we had to eat, would send my sugars sky high. One of my co-workers had seen me eating ramen noodles every day and had commented that if I didn't eat more I would die. He was partially right. If I ate any more noodles I'd go into a diabetic coma and die. What I needed was more low-carbohydrate foods. Food pantries weren't the best places to get low-carb fare. The food stamps were undeniably a gigantic blessing, but I would soon find out that even this amount was not sufficient if you wanted to buy a more healthful diet of fresh vegetables, fruit and meat. I craved fresh fruits and vegetables. These items could not be found at food pantries and meat was a scarcity as well. However, we were given ground deer and elk meat once from a food pantry.

Chapter Eight:
Merry Kwanzachanukahmass!

Christmas 2003 almost didn't happen for my kids. There was absolutely no way I could buy any presents for them. We had quit going to garage sales because even they were too expensive. Goodwill stores were completely out of reach. The dollar store might as well have been Neiman Marcus! In truth, if it was more than twenty-five cents we weren't buying it no matter what it was! Money was honestly that tight!

I wanted to give up. A stay in a quiet little mental hospital sounded all too good about right now. Could someone just take care of me for a few months? I desperately needed someone to tell me everything was going to be okay.

I dreamed of a vacation on a warm tropical island. After a day of fun at the beach I would return to my posh hotel room. I'd shower. Then I'd dine on the finest foods available. We'd go see some live entertainment. Perhaps, I'd spend the evening in the hotel pool. Yes, I'd be the guest of honor at the pool party. The pool would be heated, of course. Many beautiful decorations and brightly colored lights would surround the pool area. Attendants would be available all night to bring me towels. They'd also serve complementary refreshments, poolside. A reggae band would be playing upbeat dance music, in my honor, nearby. I'd join in the dancing later. There would also be a hot tub with a natural waterfall. In the morning, I'd awaken underneath a smooth, down-filled comforter made of white silk. My bed frame would be made of gold, encrusted with diamonds. I'd have breakfast in the swank hotel restaurant. A giant, crystal chandelier would hang from the ceiling. Then, I'd go to the spa and be pampered. A full body massage and a facial would be lovely. My benefactor would insist that I take it easy and relax. They'd encourage me to go horseback riding or deep sea fishing. Perhaps, I'd rather go parasailing or take a helicopter tour. They'd procure the tickets for any event I desired to partake in. Money was no object. All I had to do was speak the word and it would be mine. They'd insist that, "I'd been through too much." They would take care of everything from here on out. My task was simply to enjoy myself. Yep, I was losing it.

    I was just thankful that Sara was 17 and Little Jon was 14 years old. At least they understood why there would be no presents. The $1,000.00 a month I made in unemployment was pretty much eaten up by our $800.00 house payment! A younger child would have just thought that Santa Claus hated them! I told my kids that if anyone asked why we weren't doing presents this Christmas to tell them we had turned Jewish. I toyed with the idea of making a menorah and at least learning about the Jewish holiday as an alternative to Christmas. I could pull the Chanukah story off the Internet. It was still Bible based so that would be good. Best of all, there was no Santa Claus and it hadn't been commercialized. I hadn't considered the fact that gifts are received for Chanukah, too, eight days of presents!

    Kwanzaa wouldn't work either. I was fairly certain that Kwanzaa celebrations had presents attached to it somehow. Little Jon was in favor of celebrating any holiday that involved gifts. Little Jon suggested that we should celebrate them all! This would be to make up for lost time no doubt. Sometime we'll have to celebrate an old-fashioned Kwanzaachanukahmas. Oh, Bah! Humbug!

    We were more Jehovah Witness material, I mused. Jehovah

Witnesses didn't do Christmas or birthdays, either. Now this was a veritable religion for poor people! There would be no need to explain to your children why they couldn't have a birthday party or any Christmas presents. For some reason, I'm not really sure why, God didn't want them to have a party or presents. How could you argue with that?

We hadn't been able to have a birthday celebration for anyone in our house for years because we were always so financially strapped. As a matter of fact, we'd customarily postponed birthdays until I could get paid or have a few dollars freed up on a paycheck. Sometimes, we would postpone birthdays for a week or two. Other times, it would be a month before I could afford to take the birthday person out to eat and buy a small present. Jon and I also postponed our anniversaries indefinitely.

I was bound and determined to try and have a Christmas somehow. I scoured the free stores for anything that might pass as a present. Free stores are terrific places where the poor can get hand-me-downs totally free of charge. Free stores are very similar to Goodwill or Salvation Army stores. Our favorite free store was St. Martin DePorres in Springfield. We were allowed to go "shopping" there once a month. We shopped on Saturday mornings because I had to work during the week. St. Martin DePorres was wonderful to us. An elderly nun sat behind a desk near the front door. Sometimes she or one of the other workers would seem just the slightest bit short with us, but they had a rough job to do. By the same token, I had seen unappreciative people be nasty to her. She would ask to see some identification. I'd show her my driver's license. Then she would ask how many children and how many adults I was shopping for. That's all that it took and we were in. Once inside the store, there were plenty of dress clothes for ladies. There were dresses of all kinds. On any given day I could find sundresses, blue jean dresses and skirts, casual wear, formal wear, and elegant items. One of Sara's prom dresses even came from St. Martin DePorres! There were blazers with matching skirts. In one section there were tons of sweaters for every day wear and special occasions as well as shirts suitable for the office. The Cedar Chest, an upscale resale shop, donated some of these clothes. I was able to find brand name items; Gloria Vanderbilt, Liz Claiborne, and others. In a separate room there were shoes, purses, belts, used toys and miscellaneous items. I secured several pairs of dress shoes for myself as well as sandals and casual shoes. The shoes were usually only slightly worn. We were permitted to take as many items as we wanted. When I taught school and when I worked as a debt collector I was required to dress professionally. All my clothes, with the exception of socks, bras and underwear, came from St. Martin's. If St. Martin's would have had underwear, bras, and socks in my size, I would have taken them.

Big Jon had a harder time finding clothes at St. Martin's. They didn't have as many men's clothes to begin with and Jon was a large man. Little Jon also had problems finding clothes. There just weren't that many clothes for boys and he was growing quickly. Sara didn't find as many clothes as she would have liked either. She was too petite for most of the clothes. Teenagers aren't much into office wear anyway. Sara and Little Jon needed jeans for school. Jeans were about the only thing that St. Martin's lacked.

If you had a special request, you could ask someone at St. Martin's. A special request might be for a certain piece of furniture for example. We made such a request. Our request was for a bed for Little Jon. He hadn't had his own bed in years. He had slept in the living room on a foam mattress. When that tore up he slept on the couch. He was too long for the couch and he'd wake up with a stiff neck. St. Martin's hadn't answered our request one way or the other. I wrote to them again. This time they took action. Together, with the Mercy House, a resale furniture shop in Springfield, they supplied a bed for Little Jon. I was ecstatic. Jon asked a friend with a truck to help him go get the bed. When they came back there was not only a bed, but a chest of drawers and a dresser too! I hadn't even asked for the dresser or the chest of drawers. Just when I thought that God must surely hate me, God was pulling another miracle for us. God hadn't forgotten about us! Along with the bedroom furniture, there was a big box. Inside the box was something we needed very much, towels! All our towels were threadbare and falling apart. I had wanted and needed towels, but hadn't even considered asking for them. There were all colors and styles of towels, wash clothes and hand towels. There were even some kitchen towels. There were so many towels I had to rearrange my linen closet to make them fit! Joseph, of the Old Testament, might have had a coat of many colors, but I had a linen closet full of all the colors of the rainbow. God really did know what we needed before we asked! It wasn't coincidence. God still loved me and proved it by giving me the towels I couldn't buy on my own. Christmas had come early! I choked back tears as I contemplated the miracle that had just happened.

St. Martin DePorres also had a food pantry in addition to their free store. This was one of our favorite places to get food. Other food pantries in the area didn't give out quite as much food as St. Martin DePorres. There we received a big cardboard box, plus two small grocery sacks of groceries each time. In addition, we were offered sacks of powdered milk or oversized canned goods, the kind that restaurants and school cafeterias use. These extra items were located on an old metal bookshelf for us to take if we wanted them.

The line for food was always long. In the winter our wait could be very chilly. We had to wait outside on the sidewalk because the waiting room only held about ten people at the very most. There is an instinctive "dance" that everyone did while waiting to get inside. The dance started out with our hands in our pockets. Next, we scrunched up our shoulders to block the cold air from around our necks. The next part of the dance was individualized to suit each person's style and athletic ability. Young children would run in circles or hop up and down. Adult dancers would sway back and forth or march in place. Senior citizens would stare straight ahead and stand firmly in place as if they didn't feel the cold at all.

A type of "music" accompanied the dance. The chattering of teeth provided the rhythm section. Grunts and moans to indicate the level of discomfort came next. The "lead sing*er*", there was always at least one, would verbally convey his or her sentiments about the weather. Then, several of the "choir" would validate that statement. Now, anyone in line could recite their opinions regarding the frigid conditions. A rudimentary call and response song was taking place.

The song went something like this:
Lead Singer: "Man, it's coooold out here!"
First Choir Member: "I hear that!"
Lead Singer: "This line sure is taking a long time."
Second Choir Member: "Too long if you ask me."
Third Choir Member: "I can't wait to get inside."
This choir didn't wear robes. They were dressed in worn shoes, blue jeans and tee-shirts for the most part. Occasionally, there would be someone in line that plainly stunk. Others might have greasy hair, dirty clothes, or be braless. I completely understand how these things could happen. After all, my own family didn't have water on a regular basis and bras can be a luxury item if you don't have an adequate income to buy one.

The sign-in procedure for the food pantry was almost the same as for the free store. Once inside the waiting room, an older man asked to see some identification. I'd hand him my driver's license. Some people didn't have a driver's license and they would show him some other kind of ID. He asked us how many adults and children we had living with us. If you had children they might give you candy or other types of junk food. Sometimes, if they had salmon or some other special item, the old man would ask if we wanted some. If we did want the item, we had to sign for it on a separate list. Then, we were given a number. There were several workers in the back room filling boxes. When they had our box ready they called our number. Then, they were nice enough to ask if we needed help carrying our groceries to the car. We were among the lucky ones to even have a car. They had already done enough for us. Besides, I normally had Bear, Little Jon, and Sara with me. We'd carry our own groceries.

After we left St. Martin's we'd head over to The Lawrence Avenue Church of Christ. They would serve a free lunch to the community, every other Saturday, starting at eleven. Their typical lunch included hotdogs, ice cream, cookies, chips, soup, and a drink. We were also able to pick up another sack of groceries from their food pantry. In addition, The Lawrence Avenue Church of Christ had a few used clothes that we could have free of charge. This was a God-filled atmosphere. Everyone treated us very well.

After lunch we'd drive home and unload all our treasures. The trunk of the car would be filled with food, clothes and shoes. We hadn't had time to really look through the food to see what we had been given yet. As each box or sack was opened there would be much excitement and cheers from the kids.

"Oreo cookies!"

"Oreo cookies?"

"I want some."

"Look! We got chips, name brand chips!"

"What are those things?"

"I don't know, but they are mine!"

"Hey, where did you get that pop? Was it in there?"

"Yeah, we got four cans of pop!"

"Never mind. I found donuts. You can keep the pop."

There is little that is more humbling and heartbreaking than to watch your children reacting so exuberantly over food pantry donations. Yet, at the same time, food pantry days were a very joyous time. We enthusiastically looked forward to going to the food pantries.

Hands and Heart was another free store located in Taylorville, Illinois. It was run by The Way of Life Church. This store only operated on weekdays. So, I rarely got to take advantage of their services unless I was unemployed. Nevertheless, I was laid off or otherwise unemployed quite a bit. At Hands and Heart there were professional clothes, but they also had something St. Martin's didn't have. They had jeans! They also had underwear! Little Jon had little to no underwear. As I cruised through the men's underwear, I saw several pairs in Little Jon's size. They looked new, except for the fact that someone had written their name on the waste band. *Bruce* was written in black permanent marker on the Hanes label inside. Perhaps, they had belonged to an older gentleman in a nursing home somewhere. He must have died before he had had the chance to wear them. Maybe, they had belonged to another boy. His mom might have sent him to a summer camp and that's why all the underwear had been marked with his name. Bruce was sort of an old fashioned name. I suppose my first hunch was correct. The underwear was probably from an older man. It didn't matter whose underwear they had been previously. They were Little Jon's now. I took all the underwear I could find in his size and brought it home. I washed them separately in hot water with lots of bleach. I was feeling very pleased with my find. Little Jon wasn't quite so thrilled.

"Free store underwear," he exclaimed! "I'm not wearing underwear with someone else's name on it."

"Don't be ungrateful. You know I can't afford to buy underwear. It's expensive!"

"But free store underwear?"

Little Jon stood there in shock and disbelief at the thought of wearing someone else's underwear.

"You're wearing it. I've bleached them for you. I used lots of bleach. They are clean! I'm not buying you any more. You have to wear these."

"I bet you don't have any free store underwear," Little Jon contested with a huge grin.

"As a matter of fact I do. I bleached them and they are fine!" I referenced the one pair of underwear I had been able to find in my size.

Not only had I found a pair of underwear, but I also found a bra. I hadn't had a new bra in years. Neither had Sara. All my bras were, well, lacked their former elasticity. They didn't hold anything up, to be blunt. Now I was in the possession of what appeared to be a good used bra. It was a tad bit tighter than I would have liked, but it definitely held things together. One glance in the mirror confirmed my worst fears. This was a bra style from the sixties. I had cone-shaped boobs! They were pointed! Yipes! I looked like a Madonna video! It was either this or the stretched out ones I had in my drawer. What was better? I opted to wear the conical undergarment and hoped that it didn't look as bad as I had imagined.

While I was at Hands and Heart I picked up a couple of ping-pong paddles for my Bear. He was showing an interest in table tennis again and his paddles were old, from the 1970s. He needed some new ones. These were the cheap kind, but they didn't look like there was much wear on them. I could buy some cheap ping-pong balls to go with the paddles and have a good present that my Bear would like. I had expected to be treated with disdain, like a second-class citizen, because

I was poor. Hands and Heart acted like I had actually paid for the clothes I had been given. They showed respect to us, even in our condition.

Prayer changes things, or so they say. I did a web search for online sites where I could leave a prayer request. I found hundreds of prayer request sites! I thoughtfully typed up my prayer requests. I submitted it to as many sites as I could before I went bleary-eyed from looking at the computer screen. I felt that the more people that knew about our situation the better. Maybe someone could help. I went to bed hoping that this was all a bad dream. I would wake up and have a job that supplied all our needs. I didn't care if I woke up as a male or a female. Any race would do. I could speak any language. I could live in any country. It didn't matter. I could be short, fat, tall, skinny, or an alien from outer space! I didn't care whom I woke up as, just so long as I wasn't me!

It was about one week before Christmas. I received an envelop in the mail. Inside was a gift card to Walmart for $200.00! It was from one of the Christian ministries online. The note said, "We normally don't do this, but it sounds like your family could use some help this Christmas." I screamed for joy! Someone did care! We could buy a few presents and even some food now!

This was not the first time total strangers had come to our rescue. Once, I had been in an Internet Christian chat room asking for prayer for our water situation. I told them my story. I hadn't begged for money. I wasn't like that. One lady insisted that she have my address. I know you aren't supposed to give your personal information to strangers, but we had to have help. What's the worst that could happen? She could find our house and steal everything we had, but we really didn't have anything of value. That would be a wasted trip on her part. She could be a crazed murderer. If that were the case, the worst she could do would be kill us. Death would be putting us out of our misery and that would be helping us. She said she wanted to buy a load of water for us. I gave her my address, not thinking anything would come of it. A short time later, we had a sixty-dollar check in the mail from a lady I had never met in person before! God had angels everywhere!

I had also met a dentist online who donated $200.00 to help us out. I hadn't asked him to send money either. Soliciting online was beneath me, even though I had heard of people setting up websites to do just that. The dentist said, "As a Christian, I feel obliged to help you." God was performing miracles for us everywhere, even in chat rooms.

Christmas was fast approaching. I set up a small tree and decorated the house. Little Jon had made a present for me out of sticks he found in the yard and clear packing tape. It was supposed to be a replica of the stick figure from the scary *Blair Witch* movie. I liked this movie because it was shot in a wooded location. We live in front of several acres of woods and tall trees surround our house. The movie looked as if it could have been shot at our house. In the movie, these stick figures were hanging in the trees. The figures signified that the witch was watching you or trailing you.

Sara had diligently gone online for the last several months and raped the Internet for any and all freebies. She had a variety of Crest toothpaste samples, in new, assorted flavors, wrapped up for me under the tree. I hadn't expected to receive any gifts this Christmas. Unlike when I was eighteen, this time I really was mature enough to handle that possibility. These were the most touching presents I had ever received. In the middle of our abject poverty, my kids had made sure that I had something, no matter how small, for Christmas. I will never forget these presents.

There were periods where our trials were lessened to some degree, but the hard times always came back, full force, to crush the breath out of us another day. It was like being in a vise. Just when you thought it couldn't clench you any tighter, someone sadistically turned the handle another notch to watch you writhe in pain.

Chapter Nine:
Thou Shalt Not Covet

Miraculously, in January 2004, the water table rose. We had all the water we could ever want now. It was good to be able to wash clothes at home again. This alone saved us over $80.00 a month! We could also enjoy long hot showers whenever we wanted. All the dishes in the sink could be done at one time now. Before, we might have been able to finish half a sink load of dishes and the other half would have to ripen in the sink until we could turn the water back on the next day. Toilets could also be flushed after each use.

In March, I was able to find another job. I had been laid off for five months. I had one more month of unemployment checks still coming to me, but I didn't want to wait until the last moment to find another job for fear I wouldn't be able to find one at all. Then, what would have happened? I don't even want to think about that! I was now working as a debt collector. What a hypocrite I was! I had thousands of dollars of bills I could not pay and there I was harassing people to pay their debts?! It was absurd!

What was even more bizarre was Sara's *close encounter*. I had wanted to see a UFO all my life! Sara actually had that privilege. I believe it was on the twelfth of March, 2004. Sara and Bri, her friend that lives a few miles down the blacktop from us, were coming home from the Decatur mall. It was around 4:45 p.m. The sun hadn't quite decided to go down yet.

Sara, sitting in the front passenger seat, glanced across the barren, muddy cornfield and up into the sky. At first, all she saw was a set of "headlights." Sara said it looked like someone was driving a car through the sky, rather like the flying car from the Harry Potter Movie. I never saw this movie so I had no idea what she was talking about. She kept looking at this peculiar sight. Bri watched it too. Then the space vehicle came into full view. Just above the tree line hovered your stereotypical flying saucer. It was metallic gray. Underneath the large disc was a smaller, round compartment, possibly where it was piloted.

Bri immediately freaked out and flew down the Mt. Auburn blacktop at speeds in excess of eighty miles an hour. All Bri could think of was to get home, even if it meant driving *toward* the UFO. Sara was more afraid of Bri's driving than the UFO. A car in the other lane slowed down, saw the UFO, and sped away in the other direction. Our life was so miserable here on earth that Sara rolled down her window and started waving to the extraterrestrial ship. "Take me with you! Hey, over here! Take me with you," Sara screamed over and over again. Sara figured it couldn't suck any worse on their planet. Bri was horrified. "Roll up your window," she shrieked in panic, as if the glass from the window was going to create a barrier that would save them from an advanced technology. Sara rolled up the window as the UFO took off at an incredible rate of speed.

How Bri managed to pull into the driveway without rolling her car or hitting a deer at those speeds was a miracle. Bri's parents didn't believe what she told them about the spaceship. When Sara got home she told me the same story. I believed her. I was excited and admittedly a bit scared. Still, I was hoping they would come back. I found myself scanning the skies all night.

What did they want? Sara said, "They were probably lost. The reason why they were hovering over the cornfield was because they had to get their map out and figure out how to get to Florida!" Of course, that makes sense. Illinois was too cold! If they were the Reptilians, an alleged race of aliens according to some UFO enthusiasts, then they would have surely frozen to death here.

The conversation in the alien ship probably went something like this.

"Where the heck are we and how do we get out of here?"

"From my research, I believe this locale is commonly referred to as Christian County, Illinois."

"Illinois? I thought we would be over Florida by now. Oh well, is the air breathable? Are the natives friendly?"

"The air is adequate, but they are heavily armed in this area. It seems they engage in a variety of hunting activities. The natives are still very primitive in this region. They are omnivorous. They consume a wide variety of aquatic, mammalian, and avian life forms. Their favorite forms of flesh include deer, catfish and wild turkey."

"What is that small human female doing? She appears to be trying to communicate. Is she hostile?"

"My analysis indicates that her psychological condition is normally one of acute anger and irritation. She appears to be fixated on the thought of not having sufficient foodstuffs and other things needful for basic survival."

"Do you suppose she wishes to eat us?"

"I don't detect that she has any weaponry and the inhabitants very rarely eat reptilian life forms in this sector. I sense she desires that we take her with us. It appears she wants to be rescued, possibly from the other female with whom she is traveling."

"We will disembark and obtain the female as a willing, live specimen in our earth species studies."

"What is the current air temperature?"

"Thirty earth degrees Fahrenheit."

"What the...Oh heeyell no! I'll freeze my lizard balls off down there! My reptile butt requires at least 85 degrees! Get us out of this frost-bitten, terrestrial wasteland, at once!"

This ends my rendition of how Sara almost got saved, I mean abducted, by the aliens.

Meanwhile, back on earth, money was in very short supply as always. I was only getting paid $8.25 an hour. I didn't have a second job at this time so we were hurting. I brought home about $600.00 every other week. My first paycheck of the month, plus $200.00 of the next paycheck, went to make the house payment. What was left of my second check went to pay the electricity, phone, and gas for the car. Jon was only earning around $150.00 to $300.00 a month at his, very part-time, burger job. I began walking around the parking lot at work during my lunch hour to look for change. I don't know if anyone saw me doing this. I don't really care if they *did* see me. I did what I had to do. I was desperate! The pennies the other employees dropped were sometimes all that I had to buy gas with. If I got lucky I would find a dime or a quarter.

When you are cutting corners this close there is always stress involved. One day, I was at work when I started to feel very light-headed. I must be having a diabetic episode. I grabbed my glucometer to check my blood sugar. My sugar was high, but I shouldn't be feeling like *this*. The computer in front of me looked unfamiliar. I was confused. I couldn't remember what I was supposed to say or do when I called up the debtors. I hated being a debt collector! I wished I could just go home. I felt like I was going to pass out. I would have left except I didn't have the car with me. I told the manager I felt drunk and it must be my sugar. The manager said I had to leave. They couldn't be responsible for me if something happened to me on the premises. Gee, thanks! I wanted nothing more than to accommodate them. *I'd love to leave and never come back to this horrible place*, I thought. I told the management that I didn't have a car. Jon wasn't at his burger job today and no one picked up the phone when I called home. Cell phones were unheard of in our household so there was no way of knowing where Jon was at the moment. The cheapest of cell phones was completely out of our price range. The manager said they would have to call an ambulance because I couldn't stay there. I was asked to clock out until I decided what I was going to do. God forbid that they should have to pay me for the few minutes that I was feeling ill and not on the phones. I couldn't afford to pay for an ambulance so I lied and said I was feeling better. The next time I was able to see my doctor I asked him about my symptoms I experienced that day. He said it was an anxiety attack. *Oh, really? What did I have to be anxious about?* I reflected sarcastically to myself. At least, after all these years, I had a diagnosis.

"If the attacks are frequent enough there is medicine that I can prescribe for you."

"How frequent is frequent enough?"

"If you are having the attacks two or three times a week or if they are preventing you from doing the things you would normally do," he answered.

"Would you like to try some medicine," he suggested.

"No, I rarely have attacks, maybe three or four times a year," I said.

Now, since I knew for a fact what was happening, I could talk myself out of it the next time it happened and make the attack go away. My next attack happened several months later at the Walmart in Taylorville. I was with Bear and I felt like I was going to pass out. I immediately took a blood sugar reading. It was normal enough, but it had risen from about 110 to 170 rather sharply, without having eaten anything. Feeling light-headed was my primary symptom. I grabbed hold of the shopping cart and continued to walk and tell myself that I was fine. Sometimes I had to stop walking and just stand. I should have walked to one of the pharmacy benches and sat down, but I wasn't thinking clearly enough to do that. I held Bear's arm and told him what was going on. "Just keep watch on me," I told him. "If I pass out call 911." Thirty minutes later I was tired and weakened, but otherwise fine.

My job sucked! Every day for the first two months that I worked there the managers had called everyone in our department into a meeting. There were about five or six of these meetings every single day! The main topic of all the meetings revolved around how they were going to fire us all. I believed them. Several people got fired every day.

The other issues discussed in these meetings were endless areas of nit-picking, otherwise known as micro-managing. They wanted us to collect more money. However, they limited the ways we could collect.

How did they ever expect us to be productive if they weren't going to let us out of this meeting so we can work? I wondered.

They didn't want us to have any food at our desks. Our drinks had to have secure lids on them.

We were not to have any prescription drugs out and visible on our desks.

We needed to clock in and out at very specific times. If we clocked in before we were supposed to we would be penalized. If we clocked out after we were supposed to we would potentially be reprimanded.

We were not to stand up while we were working. We had to sit at all times.

People were taking too many bathroom breaks or their bathroom breaks were lasting too long. We could not go to the bathroom a few minutes before a scheduled break or immediately after any scheduled break.

We were not to talk to each other. Yet, we were to ask each other for help when we had an obstinate debtor on the phone.

We were not to wear certain types of sandals to work.

We were letting the debtors off the phone when we should have pushed them harder. If we pushed them too hard and they threatened to sue us then we would be terminated with no recourse.

We were a team. On the other hand, we were not there to be friends.

If you missed any time from work it had to be made up the same week, no exceptions! It wasn't like we were salaried. We were hourly employees. If we had to miss a few hours of work for a doctor appointment I felt like it just should have been our loss. Why did we have to make it up? If you missed a certain number of days in a given time period, for any reason, you were fired.

Our desks were to have minimal papers on them. If the manager didn't like how the things on your desk were arranged he'd arrange your desk for you without asking your permission. We were not to hang any unauthorized papers on the walls of our cubicles, even if they were related to our job. If you needed to post some notes to help you remember what to say to the debtors, oh well, too bad! So much for trying to do your job. We were allowed no more than three small pictures of our family in our cubicles. No other decorative items were allowed. I posted an age-progression artist's rendering of Elvis Presley and a photograph of a local, tae kwon do Grand Master. My third picture was of Sara and her boyfriend.

I wanted to kill the author(s) of whatever book suggested managers be completely overbearing oppressors to their personnel at all times. What type of crazy philosophy was this? Didn't these people know that you can catch more flies with honey than with vinegar? What had happened to the modern day workplace? It should have been just the opposite! If employers weren't going to pay us a living wage they should be bending over backwards to make our time at work as pleasurable as possible. They should be kissing our butts! Lording over employees with threats and intimidation didn't set well with me. They were wasting time demoralizing and yelling at us when we could have been making phone calls to debtors.

The female manager, *Boots*, was a tyrant. I nicknamed her Boots because she wore high-heeled, black, leather boots that came up to her knees. Her choice of footwear and callused personality gave the appearance of a dominatrix from some porno website. All she lacked was a whip to beat us with and handcuffs to chain us to our desks.

As the months went on the managers seemed to relax. They no longer threatened us with our jobs on an hourly or even daily basis. They even tried to joke and smile. I knew how they *really* were. I didn't trust them not to turn rabid again. However, I no longer feared for my job.

I didn't realize it at the time, but I was becoming fearful and anxious of employers in general. Most people and animals become frightened in situations where they have been abused. I had worked at the worst school on the planet and now I was working here! Although the school had been worse than the debt collecting business, the collection agency ran a close second. Both of these jobs were severally abusive situations in my opinion. This, fear of employers, would create problems later on.

On the home front, it was only June and we were already running out of water! It was far to early for the summer sun to have dried up our water supply. Then it occurred to me. Our neighbors had filled their swimming pool up two days ago. I was irate! This was not fair! They were good neighbors except for this one issue. They hadn't always had a pool. They bought their pool last summer. Coincidently that was around the same time our water supply dried up. They also had their adult son and his preschool children living with them now. This meant three more people that were taking baths next door. They also had more dishes to wash and messes to clean. Along with the extra people and the pool, they had bought two horses! These horses must be drinking my water!

We suffered silently. Our neighbors never knew our predicament. They had been good to us. In the past, they had voluntarily mowed our field on a consistent basis for no pay. We hadn't asked them for this favor. The gentleman had insisted that he wanted to do it. "Mowing will keep the mosquito and rodent population down," he claimed. The former owners of our home had not mowed the field between our respective houses and he seemed pleased that I would let him mow it.

They had also tolerated our dogs wondering into their yard. Sometimes our dogs had not been too friendly to them. One of our dogs, Bigfoot, had eaten the lady's new tennis shoes she had left out on her back porch. Thank God they were just the cheap kind you buy at Wal-Mart and not Nikes or something. Even so, it wasn't right. She never asked me to pay for them and I didn't offer to pay. I don't know where my manners were. Bigfoot had also killed one of our chickens and buried it in their flower garden. I'm sure that the dog probably dug up some of her flowers, but I didn't think to ask. When our neighbors had had enough of our disrespectful ways they had simply constructed a fence. They never said that the purpose of the fence was to keep us or our dog away, but I wasn't brainless. I knew this particular dog, a yellow lab mix, was bad when he turned on my husband while we were walking him. We eventually had to have the dog put down. I'm sure the neighbor's were sick of us. They never confronted us about anything even though they had every right to do so. Blessed are the peacemakers. They held their peace concerning us so how could I not bare with them this one time over a little thing like water?

I'm not that virtuous! Those vile creatures had drained our little underground stream dry! In keeping with our well-mannered ways, I picked up the phone and dialed up the evildoers. One ring-a-ding, two ring-a-dings, three ring-a-dings, four…

"We're not home right now…"

Their answering machine solved the problem for now. What was I going to say when they called back? I'm sure they knew what I was calling about. They didn't return my call for a month! When they did, I wasn't home. I never bothered returning their message. It was pointless. They might have apologized for our water problems, but what good would that do? Words wouldn't fill our well. We had asked them, in the past, if they would haul a load of water for us and they had said "No." I don't blame them. I wouldn't want to get stuck hauling water for someone every time they needed it either.

I glared across the field as I heard sounds of laughter and splashing. The water in that pool was mine! I'd wait until they weren't home then I'd go over there with a bucket. I'd dip out enough to do my dishes and mop my floors. Why stop there? I'd take all our dirty clothes and some laundry soap with me!

The Bible says, "You shall not covet your neighbor's house; you shall not covet your neighbor's wife, nor his male servant, nor his female servant, nor his ox, nor his donkey, nor any thing that is your neighbor's," Exodus 20:17, NKJV. I didn't care about the neighbor's house. I sure didn't want his wife! As far as I knew, he wasn't rich enough to have servants. I hoped to God he wouldn't add a big, old, ugly ox or a donkey to his zoo! The guy across the black top from us had a donkey. I sure didn't need two of them braying donkey love songs back and forth across the street all night. I couldn't give a flying crap about what kind of car they drove or even how much money they had. I coveted my neighbor's water!

God wasn't pleased with my covetousness and He had just the right punishment. What little bit of water we did get was soon going to be ice cold! We had run out of propane! Running out of propane in June isn't too much of a problem. Sara was still able to take a speedy shower in the cold water. Showers always had to be fast even when we had heated water. First, you turn on the water and get wet quickly. Then, you turn off the water while you soap up your entire body including your hair. Finally, you turn the water back on and pray that you can rinse all the soap out of your hair before the water runs out. Sara always got caught with soap in her hair.

My approach to this whole bathing dilemma was to fill the bathtub with water. It would be like jumping into a pool. Once you get used to the water everything would be okay. Also, I would not run out of water because the stopper would hold the precious liquid in place until I was done. This idea was flawed! Pool water sits out in the sun all day and warms up. Water from an underground stream stays nicely refrigerated. I filled the tub and stuck my foot in.

"Aaaaagghhh!"

I tried to will myself to jump into the tub. Just pretend this is the television show, *Fear Factor*. If I can take this bath then I will beat the other competitors and win the $50,000! I'd have rather eaten cow brains, been locked in a bed of snakes, walked across a beam suspended twenty stories in the air, or any of the other ludicrous things they did on that show! I couldn't do it. Jon started boiling water on the stove in large pots to warm up my bath water.

Only two of the four burners on the stove worked and one of those only worked when it wanted to. If it didn't feel like working it would shoot a warning spark at you. Everyone sing along. You know the refrain by now. *It was just one more thing we couldn't afford to fix.* It took an hour to get the water to a chilly swimming pool temperature. I got tired of waiting and forced myself in.

The alternative to this freezing cold experience was to pack a plastic grocery bag with shampoo, clean clothes, underwear, deodorant, washcloth and a towel. It was also a good idea to bring a toothbrush and toothpaste. Load everyone in the car and drive fifteen miles into town. Once in Taylorville, unload at the YMCA, with the pretense that you were going to workout, and enjoy their endless city water supply! Little Jon didn't especially relish showers at the "Y" because the men's locker room was aire libre. He didn't want to see his Dad in the nude! How gross is that? Little Jon also had to contend with the possibility of his classmates potentially walking in on him. This would be hard on anyone, especially a self-conscious teenager!

Our water situation was growing more and more critical. Some days our well-produced only one gallon of water. We used that gallon to flush the toilet at the end of the day. At times, we couldn't flush for two days in a row! Sara and I tried to banish the males to the nearest tree to take a pee. Less piss inside meant less we'd have to smell. Females, we deemed, could urinate indoors. Little Jon felt this was discriminatory and sexist.

"You go pee outside."

"We are female!"

"You can squat!"

Most families think they know a lot about each other. Some families pride themselves on being close-nit. Can these families determine who defecated last by the smell and/or consistency of their dump? I can. Not being able to flush brings this type of closeness to the forefront. Little Jon's excrement has a sweet odor. Bear's is more sour. It was almost as if I had a doctorate in the study of shitology. Once you see enough feces floating around in a toilet bowl you learn who to blame.

"Who took a crap in the toilet last?"

"That's mine." Little Jon smiled proudly.

"No, I took one after you," Bear said.

"Why didn't you do that in Taylorville before you came home?"

"I took one there, too," Bear stated.

"Oh my God, how many times do you have to shit in a single day? That's four times today," Sara said in disgust. "That's all he does is eat and shit! Maybe if you wouldn't eat so much you wouldn't have to shit so much," she yelled.

When feces soaks in the toilet bowl for a few hours it tends to break up. The solid chunks may sink or float. The rest of it liquefies and combines with the stale urine into a murky slosh. God forbid if you had to take a crap and there was a foaming broth already in the toilet. You prayed hard that your *log* would make a graceful swan dive into the stew below without any upward splashes. Splashing was totally unacceptable! I had to think of a better way to approach this mess. "There are going to have to be some new rules. From now on, if you need to take a dump, the proper procedure for doing so is to drive to

Edinburg!" Edinburg, five miles down the road, is the closest town with a gas station that has a restroom.

June gave way to July and the garden we had planted was now producing a bumper crop of tomatoes, cucumbers, greens and yellow crookneck squash. I had more than I could ever eat. It was nutritious, low in carbohydrates, and low in calories. It was also all I would have to eat for the rest of the summer. I felt Amish. Little Jon was quick to correct me, "We have to make it up to Amish level. At least the Amish have the things they need and we don't even have that."

Food pantry food was way too high in carbohydrates for me to eat and live so I took a very large beefsteak tomato and an equally enormous cucumber from our garden to work every day. It was usually more than I could eat. I ate them with some salad dressing we were given from one of the food pantries. The salad dressing was called, "Seeds of Change", and it was the best salad dressing I had ever eaten. How this wound up in a food pantry I will never know. Usually, it is the food that doesn't sell very well in the stores that is sent to the food pantries. This salad dressing was so good that when I had finished my tomato and cucumber salad I drank what was left in my bowl as if it were soup. Of course, in retrospect, the dressing might not have been that great. I could have just been extremely hungry.

When I brought crookneck squash to work, I'd microwave it, add butter, cheese, maybe a little salt and eat it. I'd cook my collard greens with smoked neck bones, salt, pepper, garlic and a little hot pepper.

Buying a pop out of the machine at work was a hardship that I really couldn't afford, but I was addicted. I'd drink water at my desk while I was on the phone, but I needed caffeine for lunch. Some friends I had made at work started calling me "veggie" because they thought I was a vegetarian. The next time I got some food stamps I bought a big ham steak from the grocery store and ate the whole thing myself to prove them wrong. Amazingly enough, I never got tired of eating the produce from my garden.

The other employees would bring back McDonald's hamburgers or maybe some other grease-laden fast food. I remembered when I used to eat that kind of food. I kept thinking that they are spending more money on one lunch than I will spend all week for my lunches. Yet, my lunch is much better than theirs. Their lunch was high in fat, salt, sugar, food additives and preservatives. Don't get me wrong. I hadn't become sanctimonious concerning my vegetarian fare. If I had had the money I would have eaten a hamburger with them. In my severe poverty God had given me the best food of anyone in my workplace. Not only was my food better nutritionally, I also lost about twenty-five pounds in two months. My once tight jeans were falling off of me. The whole time I had been eating my garden produce I hadn't stopped to think that I wasn't getting very many calories from it.

My garden vegetable diet reminded me of a story from the Bible in the book of Daniel. Daniel refused to eat the King's rich, fancy foods. Instead he asked permission to eat only vegetables and water. Sound familiar? If you ask me, Daniel was crazy! Daniel was passing up some good stuff! He could probably smell the King's food cooking down the hall. I'm not sure where Daniel was going with this, but he talked the man in charge into letting him have what he wanted. So Daniel and his *Boyz*, Shadrach, Meshach and Abednego, sat around eating, tomatoes, cukes and yellow crooknecks, or something similar. I wonder if the Boyz ever wondered what Daniel's problem was? I bet they would have eaten the King's greasy, artery-clogging, delicacies any day over another stinking tomato! They probably didn't even have any good salad dressing! After a ten day trial diet, the guy in charge came back and everyone still looked healthy. As a matter of fact, they looked better than the people who were eating all the expensive stuff with the King. Anyway, Daniel wrote a new diet book, appeared on numerous talk shows, and became a millionaire. Afterwards, Daniel branched out. He became the host of his own talk show, recorded a set of exercise videos with Richard Simmons and later worked as a motivational speaker. Okay, maybe not.

What really happened was, *The Boyz* got thrown in an incinerator. Yeah, for real! The King got miffed. What can I say? They got out okay though. They weren't even singed! A fourth man, Jesus, jumped into the fire with them and was walking around. It's true! He was just taking a stroll through this blazing inferno. He might have been looking for marshmallows to roast. That's my guess. Might as well make the best out of a bad situation. I never said I was a Bible scholar, but you can read it yourself if you don't believe me!

Daniel was supposed to have wound up as lion chow, but apparently lions are meat eaters and all Daniel ate was veggies. You are what you eat they say. Those lions weren't interested in Daniel. Daniel was a 160 pound squash on two cucumber legs with a tomato for a head! The next morning, the King, who had thrown Daniel to the lions in the first place, came out to see if he was still alive. This King really hadn't wanted to kill Daniel, but I suppose the *voices* told him to do it. Anyway, he was sorry about it now and wanted to kiss and make up. I don't know about you, but I would have been just slightly irritated! If I was Daniel I would have told that no good, piece of crap, His Royal Butt Hole that the lions were *friendly*. Of course, there would be no hard feelings. When King boy got close enough to the pit, I'd grab him by his fat, royal buttocks and introduce him to my "friends". No really, it's all in the Bible. Okay, okay, it may not be worded *exactly* like that, but it's close.

Daniel and the Boyz might have been content to eat veggies and water for the rest of their lives, but I wasn't. I was mad. Somewhere in that same Bible it says, "If anyone will not work, neither shall he eat," 2 Thessalonians 3:10, NKJV. First off, I had a job! I worked full-time. I didn't have a part-time job right at the moment, but I usually had some kind of second job in the past. Besides, I was living in the so-called greatest country on earth. What is so great about it? I wondered. I couldn't buy my own food. We depended on food stamps, the breadline and several food pantries. We didn't have a consistent supply of water. I couldn't shower, wash clothes, do dishes, brush my teeth, wash my hands, mop or flush the toilet half the time. We didn't have air-conditioning in the house, or the car for that matter. I barely had enough gas money to get to work. I was in constant danger of losing my house. It was questionable if we would have enough to keep our phone and electricity on each month. We couldn't buy underwear. We couldn't buy anything we needed. If something broke then that's just how it was, we did without. We hadn't had cable or satellite television in years. The best we could hope for were two or three local channels. The sound was okay, but the visual reception was fuzzy and distorted. I lived in the richest country in the whole friggin' world! I wasn't seeing any of these riches.

Secondly, I wasn't a man! I could swear that in one of those versions of the Bible it says, "If a *man* doesn't work." By rights, Biblically speaking, I should be taking care of my kids and my home. I had to take over for my husband as the breadwinner. Couldn't God respect that? Other people had told me that if I worked I was just enabling my husband to be lazy. I do know that if I didn't go to work I would be enabling my whole family to live on the streets with no food at all. Now don't get me wrong, the Bible never said, "Woman shalt never work outside the home." The contrary is true. There were women in the Bible who worked. However, the Bible says in Mathew 10:10 that, "A worker is worthy of his food," NKJV. What was it with these starvation wages I was receiving!? These people weren't paying me enough to even eat! I was worthy of at least that much. The Bible even agreed that I should at least have food if I was working. I told God that either his Bible is in error, which I knew it wasn't, or He needed to do something. In other words, I needed Him to give me money somehow. Working for money wasn't working in my case. I couldn't take it much longer! I wanted to be able to walk into a grocery store and buy my own food like an American.

Then, in contrast, I prayed that God would help me be able to bear this poverty, enjoy it even, if this was what he wanted my life to be like. After all, in Mathew 26:11, the Bible reads, "For you have the poor with you always," NKJV. Maybe I was chosen to be poor. I'd just have to learn to accept it. This could be a very high honor to be poor. Not everyone could deal with living like this. Perhaps, my family was made poor to be a test for others. Yes, maybe God wanted to see who would help us or who would turn their heads and look the other way. God is all about testing people's faith. In Matthew chapter 25:40, regarding helping the poor, God said, "Inasmuch as you did it to one of the least of these, My brethren, you did it to Me," NKJV. My family was definitely the least of the brethren. I wondered who would be blessed beyond belief for helping us. Who might be in trouble because they hadn't helped us when they could have? I could think of people in both categories. However, we weren't supposed to keep the score, obviously. That was up to God. If this were true, my family had a slightly more elevated position in life. Could it be that we were, in some way, being used by God? We were his helpers, albeit reluctant helpers, in this whole poverty situation. We were almost like angels in a way.

No, we weren't helping God. God needs no help from pathetic humans, especially backslidden believers. At the time, I felt that no church could understand the depths of our problems. It was pointless to even try. Maybe if I were in a third-world country, yes, a church in some impoverished country would understand what I was going through. If I told a church in this country about everything that was going wrong in our lives I'd only scare them. They wouldn't believe me. People would try to avoid us if they knew. They'd probably give me some pat answer, "Just pray more," or maybe, "Read your Bible." Although praying and reading the Bible are always good ideas, I needed concrete, tangible help!

I tried to give my prayer concerns to a Sunday school teacher at one particular church we attended early on in our ordeal. He looked at my list of about eighty items and told me to pick the top two and they'd pray about them. The top two?! The whole list was very important: no heat, no water, no food, no money for house payment, no phone, no job, no electricity, no nothing! How can I pick only two?

We hadn't attended church regularly since I had started going to Millikin. Initially, the reason for our lack of attendance was that I was honestly too busy. Symphony concerts often fell on Sundays and I had to be there or flunk. As a college student I was also extremely tired. About the only time we set foot in a church now was to visit their food pantry, or if they were having a fellowship supper after church services. We were frantic for food and tried to keep up with which churches were having dinners and when.

The Rochester Christian Church had a midweek dinner every week. We had to pay about $3.00, but that included the whole family. For three bucks my entire family could gorge themselves on food that was a few steps higher in quality than what we were used to at home.

Rochester Christian also had a very well stocked food pantry. Since Rochester is primarily an upper class community, we were about the only family in the area that ever used the church's food pantry. We had great pickings and were allowed to "shop" for our own food items. This meant that we could take exactly what we wanted. They left us alone in their room filled with food and never harassed us or made us feel lesser than themselves. They trusted us.

At the Wednesday night church dinners, we waited in line and watched family after family deposit their money for the food in an unguarded, open cashbox. There must have been at least a few hundred dollars in that box. Church members put in a five, ten, or a twenty dollar bill and freely made their own change from the currency that was already in the metal container. I stared at that beautiful money like it was a T-bone steak and I was a hungry dog! Sara was eyeing the bills, too. No one would think anything of it if we just reached in and took out change for say a twenty dollar bill that we didn't possess. It would be so easy to put our hand in there and grab a handful of bills. No one would ever miss them. The church didn't need this money. We needed it much worse than they did. That kind of cash would help us so much! Oh, my God! This was a church! What sort of depravity was this? We were tempted to steal from the very church that gives us free reign of their food pantry and feeds my entire family our midweek meal for a mere three bucks? Sighing, I despondently grabbed my three crumpled ones and put them in the box somewhat, but not completely, repentantly.

We also kept tabs on any businesses that were having free food as part of their promotions. The Bob Ridings car dealerships knew how to put on a good party and fed us many times. Bob Ridings had hotdogs, corndogs, brats, popcorn, pop, ice cream, sub sandwiches, and candy. They also gave away free items for your car and free tickets to Knight's Action Park in Springfield. Knight's is a wonderful little amusement park, which was completely unaffordable for us at our current level of neediness. Bob Ridings also provided local bands for entertainment. One of the best parts of the Bob Ridings parties was that everyone had a chance to win a used car. We really could have used another car, but we never won. If I ever get to the point where I can afford to buy a car it will probably come from Bob Ridings.

Sometimes, businesses would give away pens, pads of paper or pencils my kids needed for school. We'd score school supplies in this way. We went wherever the food and freebies were. It really didn't matter what they were giving away because when you are this poor you need everything.

I knew I must have sinned or one of my family had sinned. Someone had done something unspeakably evil and now we were all paying for it. I couldn't help, but think I had to be the one to blame. If I was innocent then why wasn't God blessing me with a living wage income at the very least? Trials are supposed to make you stronger. I was strong as nails by now, but I was also becoming bitter and angry. I wasn't mad at God. God was the only one who could help me, but he seemed to hate me. I was disillusioned with quite a number of God's people though. If I had believed in karma or past lives, which I do not, I would've sworn that I must have been Hitler or some equally heinous person in a past life. No, I must have been worse than Hitler, but who was ever worse than Hitler? I must have done something horrible.

We had started going to St. John's breadline for the first time the summer of 2004. The breadline reminded me of a school cafeteria. We had our own trays. We went through a line and the volunteers served us what we wanted. Then, we found a table in the dining room and ate. Usually, we ate with just our own family. Sometimes, when there wasn't much room, we'd share a table with others. During the school year, the kids had been on the free lunch program for poor children at their respective schools. With the kids out of school it was hard to have enough food on hand to feed them. I had known about St. John's before, but had never gone. I can't say there was any particular reason we hadn't tried it out. Maybe we weren't this desperate. Perhaps, it had just slipped my mind. The breadline was filled with the most unwanted elements of society: the homeless, underprivileged children with no parents in sight, the mentally ill, drug addicts, retarded individuals, AIDS infected persons, senior citizens, the smelly, the filthy and us. It was not unusual for one of the breadline workers to come out and spray air freshener up and down the line. I felt a little offended and very embarrassed at having air freshener sprayed at me, but some of the people really reeked that much.

The breadline was also full of the working class poor like myself. It was not uncommon to see people sitting down to eat wearing their work uniforms from various fast food chains. At least twice a week, before work, my family and I would eat lunch there. I couldn't make it the other days due to my work schedule. Sometimes Big Jon would bring the kids to eat dinner there as well. On the days I couldn't be with them, Jon would bring home some soup for me to eat later. This was the best soup I had ever had! It was seasoned perfectly. The fanciest of restaurants couldn't have done better! It was literally manna from heaven, indescribably good! Then again, maybe I *was* actually starving. Everything tastes so wonderful when you don't have enough to eat. Yes, we were receiving food stamps, but they were never quite enough to buy all we needed and we were never sure that they wouldn't be taken away from us at any moment. If we could have a free meal then that was one less meal we would have to pay for and we could stretch our food stamp money farther.

It saddened me that we had come to this point. On the other hand, I was very grateful for the breadline. St. John's breadline was a true godsend for my family. Without them my children would not have had the food they needed. No one at the breadline ever asked us to fill out a form or see any identification, as was standard at the food pantries. I didn't need my last three months of paycheck stubs, like I had when I applied for food stamps and medicaid. They could careless about having a copy of our taxes from last year as the YMCA had requested to be eligible for their hardship membership. No one asked if I worked or if I didn't. I suppose they figured if you were standing in *this* line for food you really needed it, no questions asked. I try not to be an emotional person, but sometimes the kindness of others, the fact that someone cared, just made me want to cry. It reminded me of what heaven is going to be like. "Everyone who thirsts, come to the waters. And you who have no money, come, buy and eat. Yes, come, buy wine and milk without money and without price," Isaiah 55:1, NKJV. Everything would be free in heaven just like at the free stores, the food pantries and the breadline. We could eat all we wanted in heaven. No one would be turned away. God was continually bringing people to our aid! He hadn't forgotten about us.

Sara described her experience at the breadline as "humiliating, embarrassing and pitiful." I can't say that she wasn't right. As much as I was appreciative, I would have been mortified had someone we knew saw us there. This was my family's shameful little secret. After that summer, we learned that a few of the people we knew had volunteered their time or produce from their gardens to the breadline. Thank God almighty that our paths had never crossed at the breadline!

Big Jon agreed with Sara that it was a humiliating experience. Jon was very thankful and he thought the food was yummy. Additionally, he felt as if he were on "high alert" of the unknown whenever we went there. In such a place where there are so many desperate and mentally unstable people, anything can happen. There was a sign near the door that said something to the effect that if anyone was caught fighting they would not be allowed inside the breadline for a given period of time. However, they would still be allowed to receive soup at the back door.

Little Jon was oblivious to any potential danger that might have existed. He wasn't the slightest bit uncomfortable or embarrassed by his surroundings. He came there with one thing on his mind. Food and plenty of it! The breadline was very good at feeding us until we couldn't eat anymore. Most people, in their own homes, might have a hotdog and maybe some chips for lunch. At the breadline, we'd have a hotdog, a salad, a desert, some chips, a vegetable or two, perhaps a separate bread item, maybe some milk, and soup. The breadline served much more than hotdogs though. They served everything and anything they could get their hands on. If it was donated, they served it. They had hundreds of people depending on them every day of the week! If this wasn't enough there was usually some fresh garden produce such as, tomatoes or zucchini that was available on shelves for us to take home. Local grocery stores donated out-of-date donuts and bread items that we could have as well. This truly was the only meal some people would have each day and they needed to eat enough to make it count.

At home, we had been without propane to heat what little water we had all summer. We couldn't afford to pay for the propane we had ordered months ago and we'd have to pay that bill before we could get any more. As the summer of 2004 turned into fall, the water coming into our house got even more frigid. All summer long I had washed dishes in cold water. I wore rubber gloves to keep my hands from turning blue. I could have boiled water on the stove to do the dishes in, but that would have taken more time than I had. Our dishwasher had breathed it's last about one year ago so all dishes had to be done by hand. The water was so ice-cold that the hand dishwashing liquid would not suds up no matter how much I poured on my sponge. We were still experiencing a severe water shortage so the dishes never all got done at the same time. The mold growing on the unwashed dishes clung to any food particles and was black in color. God forbid if dirty dishwater was left standing in the sink. The water would become slimy brown and smell like sewage mixed with rotten eggs. Paper plates and cups were a luxury we couldn't really afford. We used them very sparingly. Water was very precious.

Likewise, trying to wash your hands with a bar of soap in freezing water was like spreading Crisco on your hands. I was beginning to seriously wonder what country I was living in. Everyone in the United States has water in their homes. All they have to do is turn the faucet and an unlimited supply of cold and hot water awaits them. This water supply is available twenty-four hours a day, every day of the year. Isn't it? If that was true then, I certainly wasn't in America anymore. What hellacious country did I wind up in and when did this happen? I hadn't approved of this move had I?

I tried to economize water every chance I could get. Dirty dishwater was not immediately drained. When we ran out of tap water, I'd use the dirty dishwater to dampen a cloth and dust. This wasn't the greatest idea because it left noticeably grimy streaks on the furniture. Used bath water could be recycled for mopping floors. Cooking was practically impossible without clean water. Thanks to the many food pantries, we had lots of macaroni, spaghetti, powdered milk, instant mashed potatoes, ramen noodles and the like. All of these things required water to prepare. I now understood, first-hand, what joy clean, abundant water can bring to a third-world village like our home. You can't do anything without water. We needed water! We needed help!

Chapter Ten:
Sara Needs a Sponsor!

It was now August 2004. I had no money for school supplies. I checked with the organization that gives free supplies to the kids in Taylorville. I was told that it was only for elementary school children. Sara was a senior at Taylorville High School. Little Jon was in the eighth grade at Taylorville Junior High. They were not eligible for free school supplies. We scrounged around to see what could be recycled from their school supplies from last year. Nothing would be new. Everything was well worn, but at least they had some pencils, pens and paper.

Jon was still working a few hours at the Hardees. One of his coworkers, who looked more like a man than a woman, was helping kids that needed school supplies. I don't know what organization she was with, but she gave us a bag of supplies. I'm not sure if she was a lesbian, a cross dresser, or just unfortunate in her physical appearance. The manager at the Hardees said that she had just always looked that way, but she was straight. All I knew was that she was an angel. I didn't care. I would accept help from anyone of any religion, sexual orientation, etc. If the guys with the finger cymbals and orange robes wanted to give my kids school supplies then I'd look at it as a miracle from God and say thank you. My kids needed help!

Sara was a senior in high school. While other seniors were forging ahead with their plans to attend college, Sara was marking time. Sara knew we couldn't afford to send her to college and she was determined not to take out any student loans of her own. After all, I, her own mother, was the poster child for, "College Doesn't Pay Anymore." I had over $25,000 in student loans that I hadn't been able to pay a dime on since I graduated from Millikin in December of 2001. While Sara's friend's exchanged their senior pictures with each other, Sara had none to give. Sara hadn't even had any pictures made. We hadn't been able to afford senior pictures. At around forty bucks a piece, I wasn't even able to find enough money to buy a yearbook for her. Then there were graduation announcements to buy and other expenses related to being a senior in high school. We couldn't afford any of it. She didn't like the fact we couldn't afford such things, but she was mature enough to understand that this was just how things were for us. I'm sure it was depressing for her, but with nothing else to do, she accepted it.

By this time, Sara felt so cast off and abandoned, "tortured" was her exact word, by Jon's family that she swore she wouldn't send them her senior picture or an invitation to her graduation even if she had these items to send. After all, Jon's mother hadn't bothered to come to my graduation from Millikin even when I had sent her an invitation. What would make us think that Fran, or any of them for that matter, would come to Sara's graduation? With the exception of Rhonda and Fran, we hadn't even received a Christmas card from most of them in years. Nevertheless, when they figured out that we hadn't sent out any invitations, some of Jon's family felt offended enough to put the pressure on us. Rhonda sent an email to my account which was intended for Sara. It seemed like an attempt to shame Sara into inviting her grandmother to the graduation. I shared the email with Sara. I tried, half-heartedly, to encourage Sara to try and put the past in the past and invite Jon's family. I assured Sara that they probably wouldn't come anyway. Sara was unmoved.

Sara blamed her father, first and foremost, for letting us starve and do without so many basic necessities. Secondly, she blamed Fran and Jon's well-to-do sisters for not stepping in to help ensure that she and Little Jon had food, water, clothing and heat during our time of need. Sara told me, on more than one occasion, that, "All of my friends have grandparents that actually care about them, take them places, give them things and basically spoil them. I don't get shit!"

Roanne's oldest child, and Lisa's oldest son, also graduated from high school in 2005. We didn't receive an invitation to their graduations either. I supposed it was retaliation on the part of Jon's sisters for not receiving an invitation from Sara. Not surprisingly, we observed that we really didn't care.

Sara had come a long way since she was sixteen. At age sixteen she had wanted a driver's license, a car and her own cell phone. What American child doesn't want these things? She just wanted to be like her friends. She wanted to be a spoiled American. I kept reminding her that I didn't even have a car of my own either. Neither did I have a cell phone. We had one car, the family car, which was given to us at that. If anyone was going to have a cell phone it would go to Daddy or me first. Cell phones and a second car weren't even a realistic option any time in the near, or distant future for that matter.

Sara had missed out on a lot of things because of poverty. When she was younger, around 10 years old, Sara had wanted to be an ice skater in the Olympics some day. Ice skating is a very expensive sport. Even with Jon working as a computer programmer, at the time, it was something we could barely afford. Nevertheless, Sara learned quickly and I was going to do my best to let her ice skate if she wanted to continue with it. She was in gymnastics at the same time. I couldn't afford both. She chose figure skating while Little Jon participated in ice hockey.

I believed in letting my kids experience many things as a homeschooler; however, I didn't live through my children as other parents did. I hated freezing to death at the ice rink, the smell of the Zamboni and the unforgiving, hard ice when you fell. I can probably count on one hand the times I've been ice skating in my life. I have no desire to ever ice skate again.

Not only did Sara have to completely give up ice skating after about a year, but she gave up many things over the years because we just couldn't afford them. She loved soccer, but I couldn't come up with the fifty dollar fee for her to play on the high school team. She played one year for the high school and after that I just couldn't keep up with the costs. It was a shame because she was good at soccer. During high school, she had wanted to be involved in key club, science club, the high school science fair, decorating committees for dances, the Big Brother and Sister organization, the cross country team, track and field, judging science fair projects for elementary students, and of course to go on trips with the Spanish club. She couldn't be involved in *any* of these things because they all occurred after school and she had to ride the school bus home. She had no transportation to and from these events. The car was with me at work and most of the other high school kids lived in town. We lived fifteen miles from the high school. It was too great an imposition to ask the other kids to constantly be bringing her home or taking her places. Besides, I didn't even have the money to help pay for their gas to come and pick her up.

In addition, Sara missed out on having a part time job while she was in high school, in part, due to lack of transportation. She tried working at a Culver's hamburger store in Taylorville, but they never gave her any hours. No hours meant no pay. Sometimes she'd go an entire week or two without being placed on the schedule. Sara needed money. She quit Culver's and tried working at a grocery store. Her friend Jessica worked at the grocery store and she could get a ride from her sometimes; however, the grocery store shorted her paycheck so Sara left that job too. I don't blame her. No one wants to work and not get paid. With Sara's learning disability, dyslexia, she took more than twice as long as the other kids to finish her homework. There really wasn't time for an after school job.

There was to be no senior trip for Sara, just as there was no junior high trip for her. As the children graduated from junior high, they could opt to go to Washington, D.C., to explore the nation's capitol for a week with their teacher. I would have loved to have chaperoned. I had never been to Washington, D.C., myself. Neither of my children were able to go. We couldn't afford it, even at the more than reasonable group rates.

Sara's big trip of her senior year was a day trip to the morgue in St. Louis, Missouri. Her human anatomy teacher graciously gave the twenty dollar fee back to her in private. Mrs. Dawson knew we couldn't really afford to pay. The best I could do for my daughter was to send her on a school field trip to the morgue! By this time, Sara already had gravel in her gut and balls of steel. Seeing the full, frontal nudity of yellowed, dead bodies split open and dissected was a picnic on easy street. At least these deceased persons at the morgue were through with their misery here on earth. The most traumatizing thing about her trip to the morgue was the stark reminder that we were still living through our personal nightmare known as life.

Sara spent her high school days trying her best to hide the fact that she was third world poor from her friends. She was deeply ashamed of the conditions we found ourselves in and the horrendous repercussions of poverty. To make matters worse, she knew that had her Daddy been able to keep his career as a computer programmer, we would have had an immensely better life. Sara blamed me for marrying Big Jon and having a "ghetto baby", as she called herself. I told her I never intended for her to grow up in poverty. She knew that she had been robbed of the life she should have had. Poverty had robbed her of a life in general. Sara was angry.

We weren't living. We were existing. We were trying to survive, one day at a time, and our survival was constantly being threatened by the next bill. Some people live paycheck to paycheck. We weren't even that well off. The paycheck had to be supplemented by free stores, food pantries, free school lunches, public aid medical benefits and any charitable organization in central Illinois, or beyond, that would help us. To put it plainly, we weren't "getting by." We weren't "making it." We needed everything!

Early in her senior year, Sara started having repeated nightmares about not having enough food or having food taken away from her. Food was a very precious commodity to us, as you know by now. I could understand her subconscious mind agonizing over it while she slept. In one dream she was in line at the school cafeteria. The cafeteria lady told her that she had to pay half price for her lunch this year and wouldn't let her have it for free. She tried to explain to the lady that she had always been on the free lunch program. She knew we couldn't pay for the reduced price lunches. They weren't going to let her have the food so she grabbed the tray and ran away with it. Sara was stealing food in her dreams! She woke up shaking, her heart racing, gasping for breath, unable to breathe and crying.

A few weeks after this dream, the lady in the cafeteria told her she owed money for her lunch. Maybe her dream was God's way of preparing her for this event. She had already seen this scenario played out in her dreams so it wasn't quite as traumatizing as it would have been otherwise. She was still in a state of shock though. The school lunch was the only decent meal she had all day. There wasn't much at home to eat. I had to go to the high school the next day and straighten things out with the cafeteria. Sara was definitely still eligible for free lunches and they erased all the charges from her account. Even so, she still had nightmares about not having food.

I was also tortured in my dreams. My repetitive dream concerned a 911 call. A villain was always after me and mine. I'm not sure of their intentions, but I'm pretty sure they wanted to rob and physically hurt me. I'd be inside a house, which resembled my childhood home. I could see the evildoer walking around the outside of the house, rattling all the doors, and trying to peer through the windows. I'd crawl across the floor on my stomach and draw the curtains and shades shut. In similar dreams there would be helicopters with big search lights that shined through the windows. All the while, I'd either keep misdialing 911, the operator would never pick up, or she'd put me on hold. Typically, she'd dispatch emergency workers that never showed up until it was too late and I had already dealt with the situation on my own! A few times she told me that the area where I was calling from was not serviced by 911. This was obviously the story of my life. I felt abandoned in my hour of need. I was always on my own it seemed. No one would be coming to help me.

More often than not there would be a bad guy(s) chasing me in my dreams. They would never catch up to me because I'd leap into the air and started flying away from them in a swimming/bicycle pedaling motion. Flying took some athletic ability and balance. If my initial jump wasn't high enough, or if I didn't start pedaling right away, I'd have to start over again. Usually, it took more than one jump to get airborne; however, once I was in the air, it was mostly a matter of steering with my arms extended, approximating wings, and gliding. Sometimes, I would be holding onto a person that could not fly. I had to encourage and coach them on the proper leap/pedal coordination that was required to get in the air. I suppose, I was a type of Tinkerbell, only without the pixie dust. After they were in the air, I did all the work. It was no more physically challenging for me than pulling someone with a life preserver through water. In fact, my companion was often much more weightless than if they had been in water. I suppose the person(s) that could not fly on their own yet was one of my kids, or maybe Bear. After all, in real life they were all incapable of independently supporting themselves at present. The only problem with my flying was that I couldn't steer very well when I flew, especially up and down. I'd often fly too close to power lines, although I never got zapped by them. I'd frequently fly too high and wind up going into outer space, unable to come back down. The potential for being electrocuted by a power line must have had something to do with the fact that our very life was constantly being threatened by lack and need. Maybe, being sucked into deep space was my feeling of being out of control and helpless. When I was flying through space there was little or no gravity, but there was a kind of suction. Space itself would take me wherever it wanted me to go, usually further and further away from earth. I had to exert a lot of physical strength, the breaststroke with my arms and rapid flutter kicks with my legs, to overcome the vacuum of space and fly downward toward earth and home.

    Somehow I couldn't help, but think that history was cruelly repeating itself. When I was about Sara's age I had naively prayed for God to kill me quickly from starvation. I had been an orphan living in an attic with no heat. Now my daughter had no heat or food. Was this one of those generational curses that they talk about in church? My father, like myself, had been orphaned as a child and poor. My mother had been poor, I had grown up poor, and now my kids were poor. Why?

Sara always tried to do what was right. During science class she found eighty dollars that had fallen on the floor. Despite her great need, Sara turned the money in to the teacher. All the while she felt half sick inside. Eighty bucks could have bought quite a few groceries. That money could have been spent on gasoline or the phone bill if she had only been dishonest enough to have kept it. No one had seen her pick the money up from the floor. Now it was too late. The teacher had the money. It was the right thing to do. The teacher would see that it was returned to the rightful owner. Mrs. Dawson took the money from Sara and announced, "Did anyone lose eighty dollars?" Sara felt betrayed. Mrs. Dawson didn't even ask anyone to identify the amount of money she was holding. A boy from the class grinned and said it was his. Sara knew that the money was probably *not* his. A liar, with probably no financial cares in the world, was walking off with the money that Sara could have had. Feelings of being cheated, anger, sadness and despair washed over her simultaneously. There was nothing she could do now, but watch the much needed money walk out the door in the hands of someone else.

I wish I could report to you that someone championed Sara's cause. I want to say that someone, somewhere, sponsored this needy child and made it possible for her to have a constant supply of clean water, adequate nutrition, warmth in the winter, and transportation to all the school functions she was missing out on. For just $20.00 a month, that might happen for a child in some other country, but not here. Twenty dollars a month in the USA doesn't buy much of anything. However, even twenty bucks would have been appreciated had someone given it to us. No amount was too small that we didn't have need of it. And, it would never be too late to help us. We were going to be in desperate poverty today, tomorrow, next week, next month, next year and for many years after that. We were feeling more and more hopeless every minute. Sara was the most pessimistic of all.

Little Jon realized we were more than screwed. Unlike Sara, he was more calm about it. "That's just how life is," he would say. The female teenager is a much more volatile creature than the male teen. Little Jon knew that the reason we were in this mess was because his father was either not working at all or was barely working, for low pay, most of the time. Little Jon knew it was wrong for the man not to work and support his family; however, Little Jon didn't hold it against Big Jon the same way Sara did. Maybe Little Jon recognized that his Daddy might actually have a disability. Sara was not so sure that it wasn't just laziness. I was undecided in the matter. Besides, Big Jon had applied for social security disability payments several years ago and had been denied. Obviously, they hadn't thought he was disabled. Actually, I didn't care what Big Jon's problem was anymore. I knew that I had to support the family on my own so I had enough to think about.

What *was* wrong with Big Jon? Well, he was diagnosed with sleep apnea. That much was certain. His doctor also said he had an undiagnosed sleep disorder. What that means is that Big Jon would be lethargic at inopportune times. Going to church was an embarrassing situation. Someone would have to sit next to him and poke him to keep him awake. Usually this person was me. Big Jon would get mad at me when I kept hitting him. It took the pleasure out of going to church. Instead of relaxing for a couple of hours it was an annoying and irritating battle to keep Big Jon alert.

When Jon got sleepy his eyes would roll back in his head, he couldn't hold his head up and his speech would become slurred. Quite frankly, he looked and acted like he was drunk! This was especially embarrassing to Sara and Little Jon on several occasions. Jon might be waiting to pick Sara up from school and he'd be asleep in the car when she came out. None of the other parents were passed out cold in the parking lot. Sara's friends thought he had been drinking. They knew that Sara didn't have anything, materially speaking, and that her father was often jobless or working at low paying jobs. We were living as if I were married to a drunk that spent all our money on booze, although, that wasn't the case at all. Sara would just tell her friends, "No, he isn't drunk. That's just how he is."

Sara didn't know how to explain it to her classmates. One of Little Jon's friends, after realizing that we didn't drink and there was not a drop of alcohol in our house, just said, "Your dad is goofy."

If Big Jon drove the car someone had to sit in the front seat to make sure he didn't nod off. He'd fall asleep at stop signs and also while the car was in motion. I could tell when he was falling asleep because the speed of the car would get suddenly slower and/or he'd swerve toward the right. Sometimes, I would see that his right eye was closed or that his head had fallen slightly forward toward his chest. This meant that, no matter how tired I might be, I would never again be able to doze off in the car with him driving. I had learned that lesson several years ago. Back in the days when we still had some money, we were coming home from St. Louis, I think it was, and I had fallen asleep. The kids had also crashed out in the back seat. Big Jon had fallen asleep at the wheel just a mile or so from home. I woke up just in time to realize we were on the wrong side of the street and a semi was coming at us!

Sleep problems weren't his only issue. When Big Jon was two years old he had fallen out of his parent's second story, apartment window in Houston onto the concrete below. He hit the ground headfirst. He had two black eyes and a fractured skull, but he lived. Amazingly enough, after he fell out the window he was able to walk around to the front door. He told his mother, "Mommy, my head hurts". After the accident, it was the opinion of some people that he seemed different, not as smart as he had been before the accident. At the age of four, his parents had him evaluated by a doctor and Big Jon had been declared retarded. As the story goes, his dad was offended by this determination and refused to accept it. I knew nothing about this diagnosis of retardation until after we had been married for over ten years! However, when I first met Jon I honestly thought he acted like a retarded individual. I knew Jon was attracted to me. I spent the next day trying to figure out how to tell, what I thought was a retarded man, that I wasn't interested in him. I'm not sure if I came up with a solution to what I would say, but the next time I saw Jon he seemed normal. I figured I had been completely wrong about him. He didn't seem retarded in the slightest. Sara is fond of telling me that, "First impressions are always right."

Jon also said he was dyslexic when he was a child. I wasn't really sure what dyslexia was, but I read parts of a book he had on the subject. I could see he was horrible at spelling and writing. In his writing he'd leave out words and whole phrases. He did this to the extent that his meaning became unclear. In one of his letters to me he had spelled the word, *telephone*, three or four different ways in the same paragraph. He was also a late reader as a child.

The longer we were married, I realized that he couldn't follow a simple verbal list of "to do" items. I'd give him four things to do and maybe one of them might get done, half way. If I wrote out the list it still wouldn't get done. He seemed easily distracted by the television and the computer. If someone called on the phone or knocked on the door he might forget what he had been doing previously. This made me think he might have attention deficit disorder. At one point he was on Ritalin and it seemed to help immensely. He started acting like any other normal adult. He could stay on task for the first time in his life! It was terrific, but strange in a way. I wasn't used to living with the Jon that was a responsible adult. It didn't last long though.

The drug gave him massive nosebleeds that ran down the front of his shirt. Jon looked like he had been stabbed. Ordinarily, Ritalin doesn't do this; however, Jon's family is predisposed to hemorrhaging because of a little known disease called Hereditary Hemorrhagic Telangiectasia or HHT, also known as Osler Weber Rendu syndrome. HHT is believed to have been the source of his mother's stroke, which left her partially paralyzed on one side when she was an infant. HHT is also believed to have been the cause of several deaths in his extended family's history. Jon had to discontinue taking Ritalin.

Some time later, it was suggested to me that Jon might be brain damaged or have adult autism. I had been discussing how I had to tell Jon to brush his teeth, comb his hair, take his medicines, put on deodorant and other routine daily functions. If I didn't constantly remind Jon of these simple things he usually wouldn't do them. At another time, this might have been a sign of depression, but at the time I was relaying this to the shrink, Jon was definitely not depressed. I resented having to be Jon's caregiver. I felt like I had been cheated as a wife. I never really wanted to be a housewife that sat around watching soap operas and eating bonbons. I wasn't against working, but I still wanted a husband to take care of *me* sometimes. The husband was supposed to be the strong one, the leader. I was supposed to be the "weaker sex." Instead, I had more balls than most men and I was a *woman*! Things seemed completely opposite of how they should be.

The same social worker that I had confided to about Jon thought I might be bipolar, bipolar II to be correct. He asked if I would consider seeing the medical doctor at the mental health clinic to get on some prescription meds. Why not? I wasn't being forced to take the drugs if I didn't want to.

"Would you like me to go in to see the doctor with you?" the shrink asked.

Did I look like I needed someone to hold my hand? I must be worse off than I had thought if he wants to go in with me.

The shrink explained, "The doctor has a really bad middle eastern accent and some people can't understand him."

If some people can't understand the doctor then could the doctor understand me? How would he know what to prescribe? Now that's an unsettling thought!

The doctor at the mental health clinic prescribed some, what I deemed, very dangerous drugs to me for bipolar disorder. The 25 MG dosage of Lamictal was to be increased slowly over time until I was taking 200 MG a day. I was also given 2 MG of Risperdal. One of side effects included increased blood sugar levels. That would definitely not be a good thing. I had enough problems with sugar levels as it was. Another side effect was death! If I suddenly stopped taking the meds I could die!

Not only were the drugs dangerous, but they were expensive. One of the drugs was over two hundred dollars! What this boils down to is, if for some reason I cannot afford to pay over two hundred dollars for the prescription some month, I die. I wasn't going to bet my life on the fact of having or not having Medicaid to cover the cost of this drug. Medicaid, like the food stamp program, was always re-determining our case to see if we were still eligible for benefits.

I don't know if I totally disagreed with their diagnosis of bipolar disorder. There may be some truth to it. I am often depressed, but it's a way of life for me now. My periods of depression, which I have had since I was in about third grade, usually don't completely incapacitate me. I don't have low self-esteem. I'm not suicidal. I've never hurt anyone else. I wouldn't *ever* hurt anyone else unless my own life or some other innocent person's life was on the line. I do have times when I have racing thoughts, especially at night. Sometimes I have trouble sleeping. I recognize that I do have periods of what one might call "mania" or being "up." I can work all day and all night on those days and never be tired. I wish those times would be predominant and not the depression. However, I think the life I have had to lead would make anyone "bipolar" or worse! A few years ago, when my doctor had first prescribed the Celexa to me, he had called my condition, "situational depression." I could handle that diagnosis. My "situation" did and does suck, but now they say I'm bipolar? I wasn't ready to go there. I refused to take their drugs.

So there you have it. We were screwed in almost every way possible.

Chapter Eleven:
Uncle Sam Saves the Day!

It was late August 2004. It was hot outside, in our house and in the car. We didn't have air-conditioning at home or in the car. We were partially spared the experience of being baked alive in our own juices by the many large, shade trees that surrounded our house. In a typical summer, there were about two or three weeks where the heat was unbearable. During those times we would drive into town and walk around the Walmart for a couple of hours to cool off. We were so overheated that we would open the doors to the ice cream freezer and wedge ourselves inside as much as possible. Our skin felt so oppressively broiled that the ice cream cartons felt only cool, not cold, and definitely not frozen. When another customer or an employee came down the aisle we'd close the door and pretend to be deciding which ice cream we wanted. It takes a certain talent to look at the ice cream and not really see it. If I actually read the description of the flavor or looked at the picture of the ice cream I'd want it. I knew I couldn't afford to buy it.

Of course, I had to look at everything without really seeing it. I couldn't afford anything in this store or any other store. It didn't matter if it was a can of beets or a bag of frozen cauliflower. I had trained myself not to see it. When I did absolutely have to buy something, for example, bread, I'd look only for the lowest price. It didn't matter if you preferred whole grain, white, wheat, sandwich, or otherwise. You don't get what you want. You got whatever was cheapest!

Most of the time, we couldn't afford to buy anything at Walmart, but we could read all the magazines for free. We had trained ourselves not to really look, or even go down, any of the other aisles. Everything, but the books and magazines were off limits to us. It didn't matter how hungry we were, or how much we needed or wanted something, we couldn't have it. Reading, however, could take a couple of hours and allow our bodies to have a chance to cool down from the heat. When we were finished reading, the sun would be setting and it would be a little cooler outside. Then, we could go home to our sweltering hot house and try to sleep. A few times, it was so hot inside our house that I couldn't sleep. My body felt like it was on fire or that I had a really high temperature from a major flu bug.

On one occasion, we had been in the Walmart and a man walked by us with his family. His grocery cart was jam-packed to the top with name brand foods. We had looked longingly at his cart. This man was the symbol of true manhood. He provided very bountifully for his family. His small child didn't have to live in fear of starvation. His wife was well taken care of and comfortable. *This is what Americans should live like. All men should be like this man. It must be nice*, I thought to myself.

Sara broke through my thoughts and verbalized what I had been thinking. "I want to go live at his house," she said.

"Me, too," I agreed.

In the tiny Hyundai Accent, we were cramped together, unable to move, baking in the blistering metal confinement that was our car. When the heat index was high, I couldn't stay in the car for more than twenty minutes without feeling like passing out. If we were in Taylorville and had to go to Springfield, about an hour's drive away, we'd have to make a stop somewhere in between to cool down.

If there was one good thing about going to work, it was the air-conditioning. God knows the debt collecting business didn't pay and all the managers did was yell at us all day long. It was a miserable place to work except for the icy cold air-conditioning. The air was so frigid, that when I stepped outside, the heat actually felt good. During my break, I could bask in the heat for several minutes before the chill left my skin and it was time to go back to work.

When lunch time came, I would walk down to the drainage ditch and watch the ducks, geese and other animals that inhabited it. Their habitat had been violated by businesses and parking lots. Just a few months before, this area was either farm land or maybe woods. The drainage ditch was actually part of a small, natural creek. I found a mulberry tree by the creek. Sometimes I'd pick the berries off the branches that hung low to the ground and eat them. Other times, I'd save some of my lunch for the geese and ducks. They didn't seem to care for the abundance of tomatoes, cucumbers, or squash, from my garden, which was my usual fare. On a rare occasion, when I brought a sandwich, I'd give a few scraps of the bread crust to the geese. This was a huge donation, on my part, to the wild birds because around our house even the moldy bread was eaten. I'd pick off the mold spots on hotdog, sandwich bread and hamburger buns and we'd eat them anyway.

The kids would always ask, "Was there mold on this bread?"

"Of course not, this is new bread. I just bought it two days ago," I would lie.

If I told the kids that the bread had previously had mold on it they wouldn't eat it. Bread was too expensive to waste. I did the same thing with any moldy cheese we might have. Now I know this isn't the most healthful thing to do, but when you are constantly lacking and in need you'll do what you have to do. If the bread was stale I'd toast it or fry it to disguise the fact that it was no longer soft. If the bread was so moldy that I couldn't give it a makeover and make it look like new bread, I'd feed it to our cats and dogs. Nothing could be wasted!

None of the other debt collectors shared my interest in nature. They probably never even noticed the various forms of wildlife that lived there. The drainage ditch was my respite. Even with all the cruelties of my life surrounding me, I still felt "rich" to have a home in the country. I remembered the hawk flying low over my car with a snake in its talons. What freedom and power! I thought about the baby owl that had fallen out of one of the trees in our front yard. We had tried to save it, but its wing was broken. Then there was the three foot long, fat and very angry snake that had crawled into our carport. Bear had captured it, put it in a cat carrier, yes, it was that big, and released it far from our home. Of course, there were the raccoons and opossums that had eaten freely out of our pets food dishes. We were lucky enough to be able to stand out on the carport, just a few feet away, and take pictures while these wild creatures ate. The opossum, with its mouthful of sharp teeth, played dead and refused to budge when we moved it with a broom handle. Although they were rarely seen, the deer left many footprints and droppings in our backyard.

Not only were the animals amazing, but the variety of grasses, weeds, bushes, trees, wildflowers and vines that grew in our yard was awe-inspiring. God had really outdone himself. I pitied Jon's relatives that lived in cookie cutter neighborhoods in the city. These neighborhoods had store bought grass, the "peel and stick kind", that came in little rectangles from a local nursery. It was a fad to have all the same kind of grass in your lawn. Not only this, but you had to spend hours killing innocent dandelions or other weeds that might pop up in your otherwise pure lawn. God forbid if the people in these neighborhoods planted an unapproved type of flower or let their grass grow just a little too high. The neighborhood association would be down on them like an owl ceasing a mouse. Then, there was the edging, fertilizing, aerating, insecticide treatments, diagonal mowing of the lawn and watering that was required to keep their fragile grass alive and competitive with their neighbor's manicured yard. They seemed entirely obsessed or possibly possessed by the evil spirit of yard work slavery. Then again, most rich people probably hired their yards done for them. Maybe it was that eighth of Cherokee blood or my Oklahoma upbringing coming out in me, I not sure what it was, but in this one area, being close to nature, I was the one who was truly rich!

At home, Jon and the kids were trying to paint the house and clean.

Even so, we didn't have the means to clean up or repair a lot of things. Our septic had been leaking raw, human sewage on top of the ground, outside my bedroom window, all summer. Along with this, the septic water was seeping through our basement walls as well. So, the toilet is flushed. The waste goes into the septic tank which is broken and overflowing. The septic overflows and the waste water seeps into, and on top of, the dirt around the tank before finally oozing through our bowed out basement wall. The floor in our unfinished basement was constantly wet with sewer water. In essence, Jon and I had sewer smell coming at us from outside our window and also seeping up into our bedroom from the basement below us constantly. We had no money to get the septic tank pumped out so Bear decided to do the job himself using our wet vac! He figured that if he could pump some of the sludge out he could see what the problem was and possibly fix it. Jon spent hours outside pumping the slush of excrement out of our septic tank and pouring the brown water down one of the shallow, open canals he had dug. We had a small septic, only about 200 gallons, but it was impossible to drain using a wet vac because we still had to use the bathroom. Every time anyone flushed, that water would then help to refill the tank. The whole septic system was antiquated and really needed to be replaced. It was a losing battle.

Jon had applied for disability payments, for the first time, in the late nineties and had been denied. We were now, very desperate financially. We were in constant danger of losing our house. We couldn't buy food. We had no air-conditioning in the summer and no modern form of heater for the winter months. If anything broke around the house we couldn't afford to fix it much less replace it. The same went for the car.

The mysterious, recent loss of $45.00 to do the laundry was a major tragedy. We tore the house apart looking for that money. The money could not be replaced. We just weren't going to be able to wash the clothes for awhile. I was distressed to the point of tears over losing that large a sum of money. I wanted to give up. Why did everything have to be so difficult? Life was hopeless, entirely too hard, and grossly unfair. I couldn't even afford to go to the laundromat and wash our clothes! What horrible thing had I done in my life to deserve this? I blamed Big

Jon. He forgets everything! He loses everything! Undoubtedly, he had been careless and lost the money. The kids were blaming him too. Within a few days, the money resurfaced in my dresser drawer. I honestly didn't remember putting it there, but it didn't matter. I was as relieved and happy as if someone had just come back from the dead.

Earlier this Spring, I encouraged Jon to try to get disability again, even though I didn't believe he would actually be approved. The first time he had applied for disability I had gone with him. Jon isn't very good at talking. He never gets his point across or asks all the questions he needs to ask. I had done all the talking the first time.

This time, I didn't have the luxury of going with him. I had to work. Besides, they'd only deny him again. What was the use? We'd never get any help. I'd just have to learn how to live like this, in severe poverty, for the rest of my life. Who am I to deserve a better life? God said, "For you have the poor with you always," Matthew 26:11, NKJV. Maybe God had chosen me to be poor. If so, God has also equipped me to handle it. I know this because He also said that He wouldn't ever give us more than we could handle, in so many words. How could I fight against God? People in third world countries live like this, and worse, their whole life. They probably don't foolishly wish for better things. They just accept their given status in life. I needed to do the same. Wishing things were different was a waste of time and it would only make me more depressed. I was doing all I could do. I had a job. I was constantly looking for a better job. I had an education, finally. Where had I gone wrong? What more could I do? Just accept it. Take it like an adult, not some whiney kid. Grow up! I'll admit defeat, accept my fate and be at peace with it.

Then, it hit me. Maybe, if Jon went by himself to the social security office they'd see what I was talking about. They'd surely see how he couldn't communicate effectively. They'd see for themselves how slow he was to respond to their questions and how very little of what he says makes sense. Hopefully, he'd fall asleep on them like he falls asleep on me when I try to talk to him. They would see how he looks and acts like a drunk when he never even drinks! Then, they'd know there was a problem. Maybe, just by being himself, Jon will finally get the help we needed.

Somewhere in all the mayhem of stress, work and constant lack, Jon told me that we would be receiving a social security supplemental income check. I no longer believed in a better life. It was a nice fantasy, but I was beyond that now. I was trying to be in "acceptance" mode. If a check came, that would be great, but I wasn't counting on it at all.

It was quitting time at work. I walked out into the August heat and was blinded by the bright sun. Hey, what do you know? My Bear was here, on time for once, to pick me up. I didn't see him at first. Then, I noticed the kids were with him. They were bouncing up and down in the car and waving frantically at me.

"Hurry up! Hurry up! Come on! Hurry!"

The kids were smiling and motioning to me with more euphoria than I had ever seen from them!

I managed a half smile. I dared not be too exuberant just yet. I thought the check might have actually come in, but I wasn't sure. It was just before the kid's school started and Jon had received a beautiful check, with the statue of liberty on it, in the amount of $2000.00 from SSI. This one check was more than Jon and I, together, earned in one month! What was this? Was it really for us? What did it mean? I didn't know that much about SSI except that it was supplemental income for the poorest of the poor. I guess that described us.

Dare we spend the $2000.00? The kids were long over due for new school clothes. Sara hadn't had any new clothes in years! But wait! What if someone had made a mistake? Maybe it wasn't really ours. If we spent it and then had to pay it back we'd be in big trouble. We decided to spend just a little of it, maybe $200, on groceries. It had been a very long time since we were able to buy groceries like other American families. If the money had been a mistake we could surely pay back what we were going to spend on the groceries. The government would have to let us pay back the two hundred dollars over time, but I think we could do it eventually.

There was more good news. The social security administration had declared Jon disabled. His regular disability payments in the amount of just over $1,400.00 would start in September! Not only that, but we were going to get around $20,000 in back pay! Oh, my God! I couldn't believe what I had been told. It was a dream. This can't be real! Had God really heard me? He must have seen that I couldn't go on much longer under the conditions we were in. Did this mean that our trial was over? Praise God! It honestly felt like we had won the lottery! I didn't know whether to cry, scream, dance or run in circles. I think I might have done them all.

Our celebration in the car was cut short for just a moment. Jon still had to go to work at Hardees after he picked me up. On the way to the Hardees in Chatham, we decided that we would drive as fast as possible to Taylorville so we could cash the check at our bank before it closed. We would cash the check before the government changed their minds about giving it to us. We were going to eat tonight! Tonight we would have real groceries, that we picked out ourselves, from a real grocery store, on our table! No pork and beans, ramen noodles, or macaroni and cheese for us tonight! We decided that we would buy a few school supplies and maybe a few clothes.

We tore out of the parking lot at the Hardees and literally flew to Taylorville. Jon told me to go the back way through Pawnee and Kincaid because it would be faster. I wasn't familiar with going to Taylorville by this back route, but if it was faster I'd try it. We had to get there before the bank closed.

There were tornado warnings out for the counties we had to drive through. The sky was dark and threatening as we sped by the small towns on the way to Taylorville. We hardly noticed the weather. It could have been a bright and sunny day as far as I was concerned. I didn't care about the tornado warnings. The threat of being caught in a tornado paled in significance to the hell we had already lived through. What could a tornado do to us that hadn't already been done? If anything, the turbulent weather just added to our excitement and exhilaration. We laughed boldly into the face of the swirling clouds overhead. The joyous and festive mood in our speeding little Hyundai Accent was like a kid at Christmas, the birth of your first child, a child hunting Easter eggs, winning the lottery, and walking through the gates of heaven and meeting God combined. Stress, anxiety and depression flew out the car window and tumbled into the ditch alongside the road.

We were free! We were alive! We had survived! We were saved! Nothing could stop our adrenaline rush now.

We arrived in Taylorville in record time. Despite my expert driving, the bank had just closed. It was such a let down. Our hearts sank in our chests. I still had about two hundred dollars left from my paycheck that we hadn't spent. Ordinarily, that two hundred dollars would not have been discretionary income to just "blow off" at the Walmart. We weren't actually going to waste money tonight as it was. We had long unmet needs for food, clothes and school supplies. We had no extra income typically, but tonight was different. If we couldn't cash the $2,000 check from SSI, at least we were free to use what little bit of pay I still had left.

With two hundred dollars in hand we pulled into the parking lot at the Walmart in Taylorville. The kids quickly filled our cart with school supplies, food, and a few clothes, still, ever mindful to look for marked down items and buy the cheapest products available. Little Jon found a coat and a belt for himself. Then, the lights went out! No...not tonight! The emergency lights came on at the Walmart and all the shoppers were herded to the front of the store to check out. The foreboding thunderstorms that had threatened us all the way to Taylorville had caught up to us. We weren't finished shopping, but it would have to do for now. We'd get more groceries another time.

I wheeled my cart to the cash registers. Ah! Yes, of course, the check out line. I remember these things. In free stores, food pantries, and at the breadline, we never had to pay for anything. I had almost forgotten to pay! I never completely forgot and walked out without paying, but I came close a few times. Sara usually reminded me. I just wasn't used to paying for things anymore. I don't know if, or how, I could ever begin to explain to a police officer that I wasn't used to paying for basic necessities. After everything we had been through, I didn't want to wind up in jail for *accidentally* shoplifting! For sometime after we started receiving social security benefits, I had to consciously keep reminding myself to pay before I left a store. I finally got the hang of it again.

When the year 2004 had started, I had mused that I was turning forty this year. I told Jon that maybe this meant my life would take a turn for the better and my trials would come to an end. In the Bible, the number forty refers to a period of testing or trial that has come to its end. Noah was in the ark for forty days and forty nights. The Israelites wondered around in the desert for forty years before they were allowed to enter the promised land. During that forty years in the desert God had seen to it that their clothes had not worn out. Likewise, my jeans were thin and threadbare, but now maybe I could buy some new ones. I hadn't had a new pair of jeans in about five years! God had seen to it that my clothes had lasted, too.

Still, I had my doubts. We had to save the SSI money. What if the promised disability checks never came? Maybe, they had given us the $2000.00, but the letter concerning the monthly disability checks was an error? I was scared to spend the money for fear there might never be any more.

Around the first of September, Jon's first social security payment was directly deposited into our checking account. The $20,000 was deposited about the same time. In addition to this, each of the kids was to start receiving around $350.00 a month! We were rich, at least by our standards! Even with all this money in our account we were still scared to spend any of it except on groceries. We went grocery shopping crazy! We packed out our kitchen with every kind of food until there truthfully wasn't any room left. There wasn't even one square inch of space left in the refrigerator for anything. There was food sitting on top of the table, on the counters and on the floors. We have two pantries in our kitchen and they were both full to overflowing. Life was finally good and getting better.

Chapter Twelve:
Debt Collecting Sucks

I hated my job as a debt collector and would have loved nothing more than to quit and go home. I wanted to be home with my kids. I wanted to take care of my long neglected house. Jon and the kids were now bringing in slightly over $2000.00 each and every month in social security benefits. This was about $500 or $600 more than Jon and I had made with both of us working! It was as if God was telling me, "For My yoke is easy and My burden is light," Matthew 11:30, NKJV. God told me that I could go home now. He had heard my cry for help and had blessed me. "They shall know that I am the Lord, when I have broken the bands of their yoke and delivered them from the hand of those who enslaved them," Ezekiel 34:27, NKJV. I was no longer a slave. I didn't have to stay at this low paying stressful job anymore. He had made a way for me to escape. Still, I wouldn't turn in my two weeks notice. After all the hardship we had endured I was scared to just quit my job.

Apparently, when God makes a way for you to get out of a situation he means for you to act. Exactly fourteen days after Jon started receiving his regular, monthly, social security benefits, I got fired. I would have had just enough time to have turned in my two weeks notice, but I didn't do it. Nevertheless, God, in his wisdom had known I was too scared to terminate my position so He arranged for me to be fired. When God does something it always turns out way better than what we mere mortals could ever imagine anyway.

To sum up what happened, they fired me on false accusations. Had Jon not been receiving social security I would have just had to suck it up and go find another job *immediately*! However, now, with an extra income around the house I was able to fight my former employer and possibly get some unemployment money out of them. My first request for unemployment benefits was, of coursed, denied by the employer so I had to file for an appeal.

October 2004
Dear Appeals Referee,

    I am appealing the decision that was made that denied my unemployment benefits. I was fired from my job as a bill collector at, XYZ Credit Bureau, on September 15, 2004.

    On the morning of September 15th, a debtor called in to say that she did not authorize the payment that was withdrawn from her checking account. I told the debtor that indeed she *had* authorized that we could withdraw this amount because my notes on the computer stated that I had called her residence, spoken to her, and set up the September payment. Ms. Debtor, insisted that she did not authorize this payment toward her credit card. I then went to my manager and told her that Ms. Debtor was on the phone and what the debtor had said. My manager said to put the debtor through to her voice mail because she didn't have time to deal with the debtor at this particular time.

    Several hours later, around 4pm, my manager called me to the back offices. She showed me the written transcript of my contacts with Ms. Debtor and said that Ms. Debtor intended to sue. She said that my notes were not thorough enough. However, all the pertinent information was included. While we were in the office talking, someone had gathered my personal belongings and had them waiting for me in a cardboard box. There was nothing I could say or do at this point to save the job.

Sincerely,
Leah Riley

This letter eventually led to a telephone hearing. The judge ruled in my favor. My former employer contested the judge's ruling. A few days later the judge sent out another letter to me and to my former bosses that when loosely paraphrased stated, *either put up or shut up.* Um, in other words, if there was no further evidence then I was immediately entitled to all my unemployment benefits. Over the course of the next six months I received close to $10,000! Had I simply turned in my two weeks notice and just quit, I would have never received this extra cash.

Now, our family's income was maxing out at just over $3,000 a month! What a difference a day makes! By a miracle of God, we had more than doubled our monthly income and neither of us were currently working! We did what any normal person would have done. We celebrated! We said goodbye to the breadline and the food pantries and started going out to eat frequently. We even ate at the more expensive places like Ryan's Steak House, The Texas Roadhouse, and the big Chinese buffets.

We were now able to buy clothes! Most of our clothes were so threadbare and old that literally everything had to be replaced from underwear to shoes, bras, dresses, shirts, and pants. The material on Sara's jeans had become so thin that they weren't even worth giving to Goodwill. My jeans were nearly as bad. We built a bonfire in the backyard and burned the rags that we had once worn. What clothes we had that weren't literally falling apart at the seams were usually either too tight or too loose. Everything we wore came from free stores and free stores don't have dressing rooms. So, we wound up with a lot of clothes that just didn't fit quite right. At the time, we didn't care. We had been beggars so we had not been choosers. We were very happy to have had all the free clothes that were given to us whether they fit right or not. Sara was still scared to spend money on clothes or anything for that matter. She insisted that I take her to shop at the Goodwill and Salvation Army for jeans and shirts. Personally, I wasn't that much of a martyr. All I wanted was something new that no one else had worn before. I hit up the local Walmart for my clothing needs. Sara finally came around and started to buy a few things from Walmart, but only if it was on a clearance rack or drastically marked down to like three bucks. If an item was priced higher than five dollars, Sara refused to buy it.

Little Jon was too tall to find jeans at Walmart so we had to take him to a "real" clothing store. We discovered that Gordman's, in Springfield, carried F.U.B.U. brand clothing. F.U.B.U. was about the only brand that Little Jon could wear. Everything else wasn't made big enough for him. So, with a closet full of cheap Hawaiian shirts from Walmart, and F.U.B.U. pants from Gordman's, Little Jon was set.

Not only could we eat and buy clothes, but now we could get a few other things we needed, too. Our initial purchases included our most pressing needs. We were finally able to replace our stove top that was barely working. We were also able to buy the materials to put in another lateral line for our septic tank. This meant we wouldn't have to smell raw sewage at night while we slept. Jon spent two months digging the lateral line by hand with a shovel, but he did it. I never said we had the money to hire someone to do these jobs. Jon had become quite the handyman.

I immediately made an appointment to get contacts for myself. My last month at work had been horrible. I hadn't been able to see the computer screen after my glasses had broken. I had to sit with the computer monitor about eight inches from my face just to do my job. With contacts, I could see again at last! I also had some bumps removed from my stomach that had been bothering me for years. They were non-cancerous. I also had enough money to go to the dentist for the first time in years. Big Jon and Little Jon also got glasses. We were, with great relief, able to afford to have our cats spayed and get their shots. Finally, our cat population was under control and our animals were healthy.

I even paid off one of our past due credit card bills. Still, It would take much more money than what we currently had to start paying on my student loans and the other debts we had accumulated from years past.

Some of our other purchases were a freezer that we bought for fifty bucks from a garage sale to accommodate all the food we had hoarded. After about a year we broke down and got satellite television. We hadn't been able to see anything, but one or two fuzzy local stations in years. For Sara's graduation, in June of 2005, we went to the Wisconsin Dells for about a week. This was the first family vacation we had been able to take in about ten years. We found the cheapest hotel we could find and spent around $2000.00 enjoying every manner of entertainment the Dells had to offer.

That following October, in 2005, we were able to buy an old Geo Prism. We desperately had needed a second car for a long time. We could even afford to buy the gas for the cars. That was a miracle in itself! When I had been a debt collector, our car always used to be sitting on "E" for empty. Currently, it was always on "F" for full. Little Jon said we were real "F'ers" now. Somewhere along the line I began to relax and had ceased to automatically scour parking lots for pennies that could be used for emergency gas money.

In the fall of 2005 we were able to pay around $2500 for Sara to start attending Lincoln Land Community College. We had filed the student financial aid form too late to get much financial assistance. Nevertheless, the fact that we had the money to pay the tuition bill was still a big shock to us. How could we be so fortunate?

My telephone bill and electric bill were now being paid on time every month. The house payment was caught up too. By Christmas 2005, all of us owned the cheapest Trac phones we could find at Walmart. We had gone cellular! We were still very thrifty with the money we had. I never thought I'd ever have a cell phone again.

Life was so much better in every way. It is amazing the happiness that a little money can bring. I know they say that money cannot buy happiness, but I don't think that is necessarily true. If you have all that you need, and most of what you want, then money probably can't buy you happiness. However, if you have been through Hell, ate bug infested rice, shivered in a cold house without heat, done without water, and so on, then money really makes a huge difference in a person's life. No one on earth can tell me that a full stomach isn't happier than an empty one. Living in poverty is extremely stressful. Money relieves the stress of poverty. Who wouldn't be happy if they just had a huge stressor taken away from them?

My letter, that I sent out to a select few relatives for Christmas 2005, more or less rehashes everything that had happened to us since we got the disability money. I was still so annoyed at most of the in-laws that I didn't think they deserved to hear of our triumphs. I had forgiven them to be sure, but forgetting that they had, in my opinion, turned their backs on us, one too many times, in our hour of need was going to be harder.

Hi people, December 2005

This was the best year we have had in about nine years. We still have some major problems left to tackle, but the good outweighs the bad, finally!

First the Bad:

I'm still in need of full-time employment. I have been subbing in the local schools, but I haven't received any work for three weeks now. There doesn't seem to be much of a need for subs. I have been looking for employment and coming up dry. We are currently living on Jon's disability income, $2,200.00/month, which really isn't quite the income I would like for a family of four. But this is still better than when we were working and only bringing in about $1500.00/month between the two of us. That really sucked.

Our floors in the bathroom and kitchen are in desperate need of repair. You have to be careful where you step or you might fall through.

The electric in our house is antiquated and needs to be rewired. Whenever the kids turn on a vacuum, or a space heater in the back bedrooms a fuse blows out.

Our refrigerator is really on it's last leg. I believe it is a model from the 1970s and it is progressively getting more and more rust under the crisper drawers. It won't be long, I would imagine, before the bottom of the fridge rusts out completely from all the standing water. I don't know why the fridge collects puddles of water like that, but I'm sure it is a fire hazard once the water and rust corrode through to the electric wires underneath the fridge.

I still have $27,000, yep, twenty seven thousand dollars, of student loans I am unable to pay on and the interest keeps building.

We still don't have air conditioning or heating in our house. Last summer was killer. We had to go hang out at the Walmart quite a bit to cool off.

We discovered, this summer, that our window frames and exterior walls are less than solid in a few places. The wood is more like sponge.

Our basement still leaks and mold collects all over the house, especially in summer. This is bad on the asthma and allergies.

Now the Good: (Counting Blessings)

I was taken to court over a past due debt on August 26. In November, the collection agency dismissed it.

Big Jon is cleaning more around the house.

In June, we were hit by a tornado that messed up our roof, which was already in bad need of repair. We had lived with a roof that had holes in it since 2001. In November 2005, we got our roof replaced by the insurance company. If we would have had to pay for it out of pocket we would have NEVER got another roof.

We won a kid's bicycle from Walmart this summer. We

accepted the bike and then exchanged it for a television with DVD and VHS built in. There is no way we would have been able to buy a television like this in the past.

We have not visited a single food pantry since November 2004. We have been able to buy our own food.

We finally had the money to get our cats spayed. This was a big problem!!! When we didn't have money to feed ourselves we seriously did not need that many cats! However, we couldn't find anyone to take them and I was afraid to just take them to the shelter. We didn't have money to properly care for them and they were kind of ragged. They had fleas, worms, and some of them had colds. I was afraid I'd be jailed for animal neglect. I considered just dumping them far away from our house. I considered running over them with the car. We were very desperate. Well, I didn't kill them, dump them, or take them to a shelter. I am happy to report that they are all nice and fat and healthy. They have no worms and all, but one cat has been spayed. Thank God! A little bit of money makes a world of difference.

Jon bought the materials and fixed our lateral line to our septic tank in November of 2004. Our septic tank had been backing up raw sewage into our basement floor and on the ground outside our bedroom window for a whole year! It stunk bad and I don't even want to think about the health hazards. We didn't fix it before because we didn't have the money to do so. Yep, money really does solve 99.9 percent of all problems.

We won a $100.00 gift card to a gas station last Spring.

Little Jon won a giant chocolate bar from a different gas station last Spring.

We were able to buy a vacuum cleaner in September of 2004. This may seem ridicules to you guys I know. But we weren't even able to come up with $60.00 bucks to buy a friggin' vacuum before. The carpet was so filthy that the new vacuum clogged after just a few seconds of vacuuming. It had been quite awhile, months, if not years, since we had a vacuum. I told you guys we were living in severe poverty. You thought I was lying?

We were able to get trash service started for the first time since we moved here in 1996. We no longer have to burn or bury our trash. When we first moved here I don't think trash service to this area was even available. Then for years and years we couldn't afford it even if it was available.

From August of 2004 until August of 2005, we had all the water we could ever hope to use in our house. For a full year, our well never ran short. Then, in August 2005 we started running short on water. Illinois had a bad drought this last summer, that could have been part of the reason we ran dry; however, now in December, I think we finally have our water back again. Thank God!!

We are still able to go to Tae Kwon Do classes for free. Sara attained her black belt. We didn't always test for belts because we couldn't afford the testing fees. Yep, the belt testing cost money that we usually didn't have. So, even though I have been involved in TKD since 1998, I'm still not a black belt. The color of a belt means nothing to me, though.

Last month we were able to buy a freezer for $50.00. We have never owned a freezer before. We thought it would be holding a deer by now, but Little Jon hasn't killed one yet. He's a bow hunter. I'd wanted to get him a shotgun for Christmas, but hey, some things are still too pricey for us.

We were able to get a cell phone for Sara for her birthday. This is the first cell phone that our family has had since 1998. Yep, cell phones were something else that was totally out of our reach financially.

My depression lifted in October. They say I'm bipolar. Whatever.

This fall I was no longer afraid to go back to work. I had been totally traumatized in the workplace. I had some absolutely horrible experiences at work. I was literally distressed to consider working anywhere, for anyone, doing anything. This is not a good thing, especially since my efforts to find a legitimate, profitable work at home business had failed. What made me relax was having some good experiences with substitute teaching. I was actually shown some kind of respect, no one criticized me, I didn't have to deal with "bitches" on the job. I am ready to meet the world again. Unfortunately, the world I live in STILL doesn't have any living wage jobs.

Last summer we got signed up with satellite television. We hadn't had cable or satellite television since 1997ish. Just something else we could not afford. I wasn't kidding you guys. We were really hurting.

In May, I quit taking a medicine that made me gain 25 pounds in like three months! I feel much lighter now, thank you. The weight came off as fast or faster than it had gone on.

Last month, we had a meeting with Little Jon's special ed. teacher. He is now average in reading ability. He likes to read now. His writing isn't up to where it should be yet. Little Jon and Sara both have dyslexia. Sara overcame dyslexia to a large extent just by sheer will power. We were never able to get them help outside of regular school because we couldn't afford that either.

Last month I bought allergy bed covers and pillow covers. Great asthma and allergy relief at last! This also was something unattainable for us in the past. Five dollars for one pillow cover doesn't seem like a lot, but when we couldn't even buy a can of green beans, well…

We were able to buy a second car in October. We sort of call it Sara's car, but it isn't really hers. It's whoever needs it. Sara uses it the most though. Now buying a used car was totally out of the question a little over a year ago. It is a 1990 Geo Prism. It is in good mechanical shape, but the carburetor needs to be cleaned.

Sara was able to start attending the local two year college. We thought it would be free for her since we are still at or below poverty guidelines. Unfortunately, we didn't get the financial aid thing sent in by the due date apparently so we had to pay for it out of pocket. That was a big chunk of change. Ouch! Thank God we were able to pay for it out of pocket and that she didn't have to drop out of school.

Our kitchen chairs were all broken and we were able to replace them this summer. We found a nice table and chairs at a garage sale. We weren't even able to afford garage sale stuff before.

In 2004, we used our tax money we got back at the end of the year to buy a riding lawnmower. Remember, in 2003 we didn't cut our grass at all! Our grass was like four feet to fifteen feet tall depending on the type of grass it was. We didn't have a lawnmower in 2003, not even a push mower, and no money to buy even the cheapest of push mowers back then. Money really does solve just about every problem.

When the people came out to fix our roof they brought a big dumpster. We were able to get rid of a bunch of large items that had been sitting around the house and yard for some time. We never had the money to hire someone to haul off this large trash. We got rid of such things like, an old torn up couch, etc.

In December of 2004, I bought three of the cheapest stereos from Walmart. One for each of the kids and one for me. I have never ever had a stereo, ever! I love my $30 stereo. Just think, we couldn't buy a pack of gum without a family meeting on it before.

Last summer we were even able to drive to Wisconsin and enjoy ourselves for a few days. We hadn't been on a vacation since 1998. Heck, we hadn't been able to afford the gas money to get to work for the last several years. Driving anywhere out of state would have been totally unrealistic.

Jon finally got on disability and it saved our lives. We were literally starving before God, by way of Uncle Sam, stepped in and saved us.

We were third world poverty. Now, we are at United States poverty level. Hopefully, next year I will write and say that I finally got a job and we are at least United States, middle class level at last.

Merry Christmas 2005

I don't know why I even bothered to write to the in-laws at Christmas. We usually never communicate with any of them, except Jon's Mom and his sister, Rhonda, during the rest of the year and our communications with them are very brief. However, as you can see from my Christmas 2005 letter, I definitely had less anger this year than in the 2004 letter that I sent to my in-laws. I hadn't even bothered to let them know Jon had been approved for social security disability.

My Christmas letter to my in-laws 2004:

Hi Everyone,
Christmas 2004

There is a reality show on TV called *Trading Spaces*. I hope you have seen it. Basically, two women from two different families trade places for two weeks. The first week they have to live by their host families rules and do everything just exactly like the real mom would have done. The second week the women get to change the rules for their host families however they want. At the end of the two weeks each mom has to decide how she will spend 50k on their host family. The host family has no input on how the money is spent.

TRADING SPACES THE LOST EPISODE

The Jon D. Riley Family and The (Insert Your Last Name) Family

House Rules for the First Week

The following list of chores must be done. Your duties include, but are not limited to: Sweeping, mopping, cleaning the bathrooms, doing dishes by hand (no dishwasher), boiling water on the stove to do dishes with (cuz we ran out of propane a few months back), vacuuming, tending sick animals, taking out trash and burning it, washing the dog, feeding all the cats (about 12 cats) and the dog, dropping off and picking up kids at school, doing laundry (at the Laundromat cuz not enough water at home to do laundry there), carrying in firewood and starting fires, cleaning out the carport and back porch, cooking, mystery shopping, cleaning windows, cleaning out closets, cleaning out cobwebs, mowing lawn, picking up sticks in yard (we have a lot of trees), going to the YMCA for baths (cuz not enough water at home to bathe and also no hot water at home), dealing with the Sallie Mae people concerning my student loan that I can't repay (usually they call), going by the phone company, electric company and bank in person with money orders to make payments (cuz no checking account), raking leaves, getting rid of spider webs and spiders, painting rooms, cleaning out gutters, and going to work.

However, none of these chores have a set time or day to do them on, except for going to work. Work will take you away from the home for 10 hours minimum a day, longer if you have to wait for a ride. I live on Indian time. If you don't get it done today...hey, it'll be there tomorrow, and the next day, and the next day, and the next day...bottom line however is...If it's going to get done, YOU have to do it cuz no one else will.

Good luck doing all the chores when you are dead from working 10 hours a day.

In your free time, you really don't have free time, but you will go to free tae kwon do classes (wear something comfortable and loose fitting) and to free stores and food pantries. Free stores are places where you can shop and they do not charge money because they are for poor people. They are like second hand stores. It is kind of like a garage sale, but no money is required. It really is kind of fun. Big Jon can provide you with an extensive list of food pantries. Some food pantries are better than others. The bread line is where you will eat before going to work. Above all else, you cannot speak about going to the breadline, or the food pantries, or the free store to any of my kids' friends or anyone at Tae Kwon Do. It would embarrass us to no end. This request MUST be adhered to.

We eat whatever they give us at the food pantries, or the breadline, and supplement with $192.00/month in food stamps.

Sara is very busy with homework all the time. She pushes herself hard in school. She also has a boyfriend she goes out with on weekends. He is into metal music and dresses accordingly, but is harmless. Sara dresses normally and is not into metal.

Some of the staples that everyone will eat are, fresh baked bread, beans and weenies, tuna helper, hamburger helper, tacos, hamburgers, grilled cheese sandwiches, chicken noodle soup, brownies, sloppy joes, frozen cheese or pepperoni pizzas, frozen French fries, sweet potatoes, macaroni and cheese, canned biscuits, homemade potatoes fried with bacon grease with shredded cheese on top, chicken and dumplings made fresh or out of a can, grapes, bananas, and peanut butter and jelly sandwiches. As time and money permits, the kids like brussel sprouts, cabbage and sausage, spinach, asparagus, beets, canned cinnamon rolls, frozen broccoli stuffed chicken, cauliflower, and canned ravioli. Little Jon likes steak, fried fish, oatmeal raisin cookies, fried green tomatoes and hot, spicy foods. Big Jon will **not** eat cabbage, green peppers, olives, brussel sprouts, beets, asparagus, spinach, broccoli, fish or cauliflower. Neither of the kids like onions, mushrooms, meatloaf or green peppers. Sara will **not** eat fish, hot and spicy foods, and steaks or other foods with fat in it. If left to his own devices, Big Jon will make spaghetti two or three times a week. The kids won't eat spaghetti anymore because of this. On the other days of the week he makes macaroni and cheese and the kids don't really like this anymore either. Two nights out of the week you work late anyway so you don't have to deal with the evening meal. They are on their own. Good luck trying to find something that everyone will eat. I do cook real food, not from a box, on weekends, time and money permitting.

The male head of household does not work. He occupies his time doing repairs around the house. He will help out with the cleaning, but usually has to be told what to do and when to do things. He will also start to clean an area then forget what he is doing and get off task so he needs supervision. Make out a list for him, have him post it somewhere, and maybe something will get done while you are at work. If not, when you get home from work you can make him work on the list then. He has Narcolepsy and falls asleep a lot. It isn't wise to let him drive. He also has ADD which keeps him unfocused.

On Tae Kwon Do night you might eat off the dollar menu at McDonalds, depending on if you have the money for it or not.

***

House Rules for the Second Week…
Well, this part would be up to you and my family would have to follow your rules. Little Jon and Big Jon are pretty much compliant. Sara, on the other hand, may not do what you ask.

***

The Last Thing:
I would have to decide how to spend $50,000 on your family and you on mine. Every person that has ever traded places has had a hard time with this one cuz they don't know what the host family wants or needs. I would be in the same spot cuz I have no clue what you would use $50,000 on either. So, I guess I would take $10,000 of that and give you

an all out very nice fantasy vacation somewhere fun. Everyone needs a vacation I think. Then I would leave $40,000 for you to do with what you pleased. Yep. Merry Christmas!

***

In the land of Lincoln,
Jon, Leah, Sara and Little Jon

Please consider making a donation to your local food bank, Salvation Army, America's Second Harvest or the United Way. When you help these organizations you really do help people like us. The need is great and the economy sux!

Drop your spare change in the salvation army bell ringers kettle! As little as 7 cents can buy a pack of ramen noodles for someone in **THIS** country. No amount is too small. Heck, you can probably find 7 cents in the parking lot just walking in to the store.

***

The following Christmas letter I sent off to my sisters in 2004, actually informed them of the fact we were receiving social security. I don't know why I felt compelled to give them this bit of information. None of my sisters had ever helped me out in my times of need. Then again, I had never directly asked them for help. I guess I hadn't wanted to appear weak to them. Call it pride if you must. I suppose the older I get the more I realize that they were just kids themselves when we lost our parents. They must have had it rough in a lot of ways, too. I'm not exactly sure how they suffered, but I'm positive that they must have.

***

A portion of my 2004 Christmas Letter to my sisters:

Hi,
We are a little bit better off now. Jon got his disability started in August 2004.

Sara graduates this year from high school. I keep telling her if she figures out how to survive to let me know.

At least with Jon having an income now, I am more free to do things.

We are doing great for now.

The last time I bought jeans was about five years ago. It was funny buying jeans because they are all made out of stretchy material now. I wear a size smaller in these new kind of jeans.

We also found out that the video store rents DVD's now and not VHS. It has been that long since we have even been able to rent a movie. We paid off our late fees, from who knows how long ago, while we were there as well.

We bought propane so we could have heated water again. None of us liked going to the YMCA to take showers. It was a real novelty to take a shower in your own house again.

I managed to pay off a Sears credit card from about four years ago.

We can now go to the grocery store any time we please and get anything we need and really, most of what we want. I remember going in to the grocery store with ten bucks and telling the kids, "we all have to agree on one thing for dinner because this is all I have." We used to wait in lines for food handouts at food pantries.

I would love to get a decent job to compliment his disability money. If I could get a job that paid $2,000/month I could have all my debts paid off in short order.

We have indulged in a few luxuries…okay, quite a few luxuries. We have eaten out quite a bit. We bought a new computer at Walmart for Christmas, $600. I was surprised that the prices of electronics, and well everything, is so low now compared to what it used to be…

Author's Note:
Now What?

Well, time goes on, and with it comes more miseries. Sara totaled the Geo Prism after just nine months. Sara went down a twenty foot embankment at 55 miles per hour, about a mile from our house, and rolled the car. The front passenger's side hood was seriously dented where she had angled into the ditch. The trunk on the driver's side was smashed, the taillight was demolished and the tire on that side was blown. The windshield was folded and shattered. The rearview mirror on the driver's side was torn off and there were bumps and scrapes on the sides of the car. No one actually saw the accident, but from the evidence, it appeared that she cartwheeled the car. We didn't have full coverage on the Prism so we weren't going to get a dime from the insurance company.

There were no other cars involved, thank God. The road conditions were fine. It was a bright and sunny afternoon. Apparently, she slipped on some gravel and simply lost control of the car. The police officer said that about three other people had wrecked in that same place. One of the others, a girl, had died in that same spot a few years back. Sara suffered minor cuts and bleeding from the broken glass, whiplash, and some impressive bruises. Sara refused to go to the hospital or see Dr. McClintock because she had no medical insurance. As a matter of fact, she was back at work the next morning at 4:00 a.m. Luckily, Sara had a job at McDonald's and was able to buy another cheap used car to replace the Geo. Of course, this took everything that Sara had saved in the bank. Sara knew that she had to painstakingly rebuild her meager savings account again and that wasn't going to happen if she didn't work. Now, that's the daughter I raised! We have "balls" in this family!

Jon called his mother to tell her what happened. We didn't need his mother's help this time, but it would be interesting to see her response. I don't know why he even bothered to call. Even if we actually needed help, family would probably not be the ones to ask.

Fran sent the following letter to us:

> August 8, 2006
> Dear Jon,
> I am giving each of you $50.00 for your birthdays 2006 and March 1, 2007. And one for good luck, that Is $250.00 in all…Dr. Phil on NBC every weekday afternoon says, "If you really love your children you won't give them any money except in extreme emergencies!" So, I really shouldn't be giving you money…

Now, I must admit, that I have watched Dr. Phil's program on television a few times. I don't agree with half of what he says, but occasionally he makes a good point. The man just irks me. Now, I don't know for a fact if Dr. Phil actually said that on one of his programs, but it does sound like something he would say. And I don't necessarily disagree with this one statement if he did indeed say it; however, after having read this book, I'll let you decide. If my whole life hasn't been an extreme emergency, then I don't know what an emergency is. Can I get an Amen?

What was left of Jon's back pay from social security was completely gone after we had bought the Geo, and paid for Sara's tuition, in the fall of 2005. I hadn't been able to find full-time employment since September of 2004, so we were starting to feel the twinges of poverty again. We were living month to month, but at least we were not as desperate as we had been before Jon had received his disability checks. We never went back to a single food pantry or free store.

In January 2006, I noticed that our septic tank was messed up again. I still don't know what I'm going to do about the septic. We really need a whole new system. I had one man give me an estimate of $5,000.00 to replace the system. Maybe, one of these days, I will eventually have a job the pays enough to afford that kind of thing. I'm not giving up hope yet.

About four months after we bought our second hand refrigerator, it died. It was a nice side by side with ice and water on the door. Now, we are back to our leaky, rusted, '70s yellow, beat-up fridge, with the missing handle and shelves.

In May 2006, we ran out of propane so we no longer had hot water. Now I could have ordered more, but I didn't. I don't know why I didn't order more. Perhaps, hot water was no longer a need for me. Summer was coming up soon and hot water wasn't necessary during the summer. In addition, I could now bug bomb the basement and finish painting it without worrying about turning off the pilot light to the water heater. Besides, I had learned to take a bath, refugee style, out of a large pot of water which was warmed on the stove. It worked fine and we saved lots of water. Sara, the girl who invented the ice cold shower, started going back to the YMCA for showers. I'll probably get propane when autumn comes.

I had two part-time jobs in the summer of 2006. I loved both of my jobs. I thought they were great! The work was meaningful and fulfilling, even if it didn't pay much. There were good people at both of my jobs and we all got along well. One of the jobs, an answering service in Springfield, laid me off before I had even worked their one full month! The other job just quit paying me for the hours I did work. I immediately launched another major job hunt, without much success.

We were never able to afford a new air-conditioning or heating unit.

So, we get to be miserable, in the heat and humidity of summer, for awhile longer.

Okay, so, this isn't the happily ever after you were expecting? Hey, what can I say? I'm real. At least we are a little better off. Things are improving.

I actually got hired to teach part-time at a really great school. It's a start. Besides, this part-time position pays as much as most of the crappy jobs I've worked at full-time. However, the reality is that I really do need more money to pay for all the stuff we still need. Now all I have to do is find another part-time job and I'll have pieced together one full-time job out of two part-time jobs. Our life is still complicated. Nothing is ever easy, but hopefully we are getting somewhere now. For now, I'll have to leave you with this uncertain, yet hopeful, ending.

Finally, when God wrote His bestseller, the Bible, He said, "For I testify to everyone who hears the words of the prophecy of this book: If anyone adds to these things, God will add to him the plagues that are written in this book," Revelation 22:18, NKJV.

I wouldn't wish the "plagues" found in *my* book on anyone!

Printed in the United States
87106LV00004B/154/A